NOTES

JOSEPH MALARA

BOXING
INSTRUCTION
AND MORE !

THE BIBLE ON HOW TO BOX

"THE BOOK TO BEAT ALL OTHERS"

INSTRUCTION AND MORE!

FOR FITNESS, HEALTH, STREET SELF DEFENSE, AMATEUR & PROFESSIONAL WORLD CHAMPIONSHIP BOXING TITLES

ISBN: 9798617735620

Written by Joseph Malara

Contents edited by Aimee Malara

Cover design by Aimee Malara

I wanted to smile, but I was on my last rep of 8 with 225 pounds in each hand.

Written by Joseph Malara

Drawings by Chad Ludwig

Contents edited by Aimee Malara

Cover design by Aimee Malara

Malara Has Written

"God's Clarity Through Poetry"

"Digging Deeper into God's Truth Defines a Christian"

"God's Clarity Through Poetry 2"

And This Book

"The Bible On How To Box"

Introduction

Back in 1985 I wanted to create a video on *How to Box*, so I started filming it. I sought some help, so I invited Mr. Ray Arcel to lunch. Ray was one of the greatest Boxing trainers of all time; he trained 20 world champions, from Ezzard Charles to Roberto Duran! I picked him up at his Manhattan apartment for a lunch appointment we made days earlier. I brought him to a Queens Dinner called Mark Twain, close to where I lived at that time. I showed him a script I wrote which I had copy written to be the first *How to Box* video. That was my plan; which later developed into this book you hold in your hand. Ray Arcel took about 15 minutes to look over it, he loved the script and said, "I like the way you explained the punches, it's put together well, it's excellent, but Joseph, it would be hard to teach boxing on a video, it has never been done."

I replied, "I know, that's why I want to make this training video on *How to Box*, with your help," he said, "Okay, I will help you, let me know how I can help." By the time I found the time to fully commit to that project, Mr. Arcel sadly passed away. My procrastination was evident and very, very regrettable.

Let me give you some of my background. I had boxing gloves on my hands at age 8. We lived in Harlem, New York City. I could never run that fast, so I learned to fight. Later at age 13 we moved to the projects in Woodside Queens. I was training more seriously for boxing at age 12 by age 15 I would take a bus and train each night at a boxing gym. I remember telling my parents that I would get them out of the projects by fighting; which never happened; as I hit the speed bag and heavy bag for countless hours at end; both were set up in my bedroom! I boxed amateur and was undefeated. I went on and including my Boxing I studied five different styles of fighting: Boxing (*American*), and in Martial Arts, Taekwondo (*Korean Karate*), Tai Chi Chuan (*Chinese Kung Fu*), Goju-Ryu (*Japanese Karate*) and I dabbled in Jeet Kune Do (*Bruce Lee's style*) all this over a twenty year span.

This did take my eyes off of boxing for a while. Going through all that, I realized one day while my Sensei (*Teacher*) asked me to spar him in front of the whole class, at that time he was a Master and I was nearly a brown belt in that discipline, but belts are only to hold up your pants. I found keeping within the boundaries of his style, which I was at that time learning Goju-Ryu. I was at a huge disadvantage, so I changed up; I used Taekwondo. I boxed and kick boxed, and my

Sensei got furious. He yelled, "Stop, do not use any other style here but what I teach you." I realized he could not beat me, and adapting is what's needed to win in hand to hand combat. So my background has taught me, to use what works. Don't buy into any one style; they are all rigid and restricting. There are hard and soft styles, but all have their limitations; katas are like short plays, its memorizing techniques. Which means you will lean on them when needed, but that is not always true in real life. Freedom from all styles is best, but adherence to your surroundings in conjunction with a strong skillful fighting foundation, one which permits protection and allows you to attack as well; such is boxing, done right.

With this book you will learn such a foundation; of which to defend your-self and to attack from. Learning to balance oneself and launch attacks with confidence is what's needed. This can only be accomplished by understanding the basics, which this book is heavy on. I always had a real desire to be a boxing world champion myself; a dream, so I trained from 1994 to 1997. I trained 3 years to make a comeback in Boxing. My efforts found me preparing to spar Roy Jones and turn pro. Days before meeting him and doing so, I was driving in a corvette which I owned only 10 minutes. While driving it home on the highway, I got hit from behind by an 18 wheeler Mac Truck fill of sand.

That was the conclusion of my dream, of owning such a small car and my dream of being a world champion boxer; that's what I felt at that time. I was able to walk out of that accident by the Grace of God! All 4 wheels were off the car, and its steering wheel was bent in my hands!

I remember both the paramedic and ambulance driver remarked that I was in such great shape. Yes, I was in the best shape of my life. I guess God was telling me not to turn pro; He had other plans for me, which today I understand. So, I never followed up to spar or even met Roy. To make a long story short; a year later being a very persistent person, I returned to the gym. Restarted my training, but while hitting the heavy bag, it was noticeable that I wasn't throwing my right hand as often as I needed too, I retained soft tissue damage. My trainer remarked, "Joseph you are training to be the very best in the entire world and having any limitations at all will hinder such goals greatly." I knew he was right…

While at that gym one day, the well-known boxing trainer Teddy Atlas came by; he was training Shannon Briggs for an upcoming fight. Teddy took a look at my book (this book) and really liked it, he asked why did I write this, what gave me such passion? I told him boxing has been my passion since my dad brought boxing gloves into our home when I was 8 years old. I would study back then 8mm and super 8mm fight films on a projector which had no sound. I would study all the old fighters' their moves and imitate their moves precisely and I would practice them for many, many hours. I studied fighters from Jack Johnson, Jersey Joe Walcott, Rocky Marciano to Muhammad Ali, and countless others in all weight classes. It was my passion and joy. I spent years doing that. Teddy seemed pleased with my answer, and then Teddy and I took some pictures. Michael Moore was there with Teddy as well, I asked Michael if I could create a sculpture of his hands. This was something I was involved in back then. I tried to think big and wanted to open a Museum which would bring remembrance to our past, honoring people who made a difference. I told Michael Moore, what I was planning to do. He said, "No not interested," I said, "I would create one for him as a gift and another for me, towards my efforts and they cannot be massed produced or even copied in any way." We talked a while, as he had his entourage with him that day.

This was the gym I was training in at that time in Tampa Florida. So I asked Michael if he was afraid to fight Mike Tyson. At this time Michael Moore just recently lost his Heavyweight title to George Forman. He said, "I am not afraid of nobody," I replied, "you are afraid of something" he retorted, "really what?" I said, "You're afraid to let me create a cast sculpture of your hands", he got up and got really mad at me, so I got up and said, "What, are you going to hit me now?" That's when his body guard stepped in…Remember, I was in training and in my heart I believed at that time I could beat anyone in the world. I was very happy I didn't get into a scrap with Michael that day, thinking back now he outweighed me by 50 pounds! God is good! A few years after from 1995 to 2000 I had created castings of Carmen Basillo, Jackie Chan, Jack LaLanne and Halle Berry's hands and many others which are all immortalized in solid stone. But throughout the following years, my efforts although diligent and consistent; sadly that Museum never got off the ground.

This is the 2nd edition of this Boxing book; it's slightly updated as the first edition went unpublished. I only gave copies to friends and other fighters I knew. I pray this edition finds its way around the world and helps many to learn the fundamentals of the art of Boxing, along with its advanced techniques; and with this book in hand, perhaps YOU can accomplish a dream, I once had.

Acknowledgments

I first put this book together in 1989 re-written in 1994 and completed it a year later, now in 2020 updated it and it's finally published. All the Glory goes to God and to Jesus my Lord and Savior, along with The Holy Spirit for allowing me Life, and giving me inspiration to write anything at all. I also want to thank my gorgeous wife Aimee, for her much devoted time, constant support and ongoing love; she is a Godsend and priceless. This book is a testimony, testifying it's never too late to re-live and to re-write ones passions. To take something once written and almost forgotten, off a dusty shelf; re-birth it, and share it with those who can use it, learn from it, teach from it and benefit from it. God is Good!

For personal instruction, counseling, consultation, supervision, advanced level training, further information or questions pertaining to your current training, the contents of this book or information not referred to herein, please feel free to email the author personally.

JosephMalara@yahoo.com

To keep up with all books written by Joseph Malara visit www.JosephMalara.com

THE BIBLE ON HOW TO BOX

"THE BOOK TO BEAT ALL OTHERS"

FOR FITNESS, HEALTH, STREET SELF DEFENSE

AMATEUR & PROFESSONAL WORLD CHAMPIONSHIP

BOXING TITLES

Chapter 1

* BASICS & FUNDAMENTALS *

Is Boxing as easy as one, two, three? First you must learn to master the knowledge required. Second, turn this knowledge into precise movement through concentrating and focusing on correct form, and third, using this form to launch sharp rapid attacks and swift retreats.

Before attempting any of the moves or training techniques in this book, get a check-up by your physician, have him state that you're fit to train and go through physical exertion. Use this book as a meaningful workbook, mark in it, highlight it, and study it as you would The Bible, God's Word.

Remember to know yourself and your capabilities and do not expect too much too soon. Some people are born with good physiques, great speed, timing and seemingly endless endurance. That's fine, but boxing is a <u>skill</u> taught by <u>many</u> lessons before it can be mastered, once mastered you will seem invincible to the eye of the unskilled fighter. Proper conditioning combined with the proper boxing skills will 99 out of 100 times, beat the much stronger or genetically gifted opponent, not possessing these qualities, "I believe champions are made, not born, so let's start the making!

The proper method in <u>making a fist</u> (Note: Fig. #1), hand is closed tight, with thumb rolled over the first two fingers. The top of your hand is flat (Note: Fig. #2), the thumb side of your hand is flat (Note: Fig. #3), outer part of your hand is also flat, keeping a straight line with the forearm (Note: Fig. #4). Punches are delivered with the fist as shown (Note: Fig. #5), as with all boxing punches the fist should land squarely using <u>all four</u> knuckles of that punching hand, making certain that there's no bending of the wrist in any direction (Note: Fig. #6), on what <u>NOT</u> to do; your hands are your tools for contact, make certain your hands are always tight right <u>before</u> delivery.

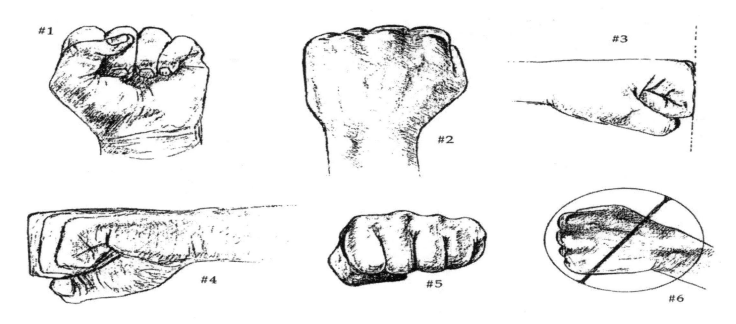

Placing both hands, as shown (Note: Fig. #7), (throughout this book we are going to assume you are a right-handed person). This is called an **orthodox** fighter, one who leads with his left, keeping his power hand behind the lead hand. This is usually a right-handed person. A left-handed person is called an "un-orthodox" fighter or also known as a **"southpaw"** one who leads with his right hand (Note: Fig. #8) for those of you, who are southpaw boxers, reverse all boxing procedures in this book, leading with your right hand.

Remember, if you are a right-handed boxer or (orthodox) fighter, facing a left-handed boxer, (southpaw) or un-orthodox fighter and there is awkwardness for you, it should be just as awkward for him. Except for the fact that the left-handed, or as we will now refer to as the southpaw fighter will be more accustomed to the sort of opposition he encounters by fighting mostly right-handed fighters; what we will now refer to as orthodox fighters. All orthodox fighters must practice and experience sparring southpaw fighters, as well, more on this later.

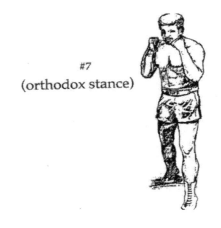

#7
(orthodox stance)

#8
(south-paw stance

This boxing stance (Note: Fig. #9), is called the on-guard ready position or defensive & offensive position, we will refer to it as the **on-guard position**. Your chin is tucked slightly into your chest; your elbows are in front of your body protecting your sides and body. Hands held in front of your face about earlobe level protecting your chin and face. You are partially contracted at the waist, your left leg is in front of you, giving your opponent a sort of side view; this is the safest position (Note: Fig. #10, #11). As a "defensive" position you will be able to block your opponents' punches protecting yourself and delivering your own punches from the same position making this on-guard position also an "offensive" position. A good on-guard position should reveal what a good poker player face reveals…nothing…no faults, no hint of what is to come.

#9
(front view)

#10
(right side view)

#11
(left side view)

While in the on-guard position, your legs should be directly under your body, too wide a stance may give you more power but at the cost of speed and efficient movement (Note: Fig. #12). Too narrow a stance may give you speed, but no balance and power (Note: Fig. #13). What's needed is to keep feet directly under your body, a medium distance apart, pointing lead leg (your left) toward your opponent and in-between opponents' legs. This will keep you in both offensive and defensive range (Note: Fig. #14) standing at an angle towards your opponent, showing him mostly your left hand (lead hand). If you expose more, you will be an easy target and have little to no balance (Note: Fig. #15) on what <u>NOT</u> to do.

Think of Zorro leading with his sword, with you, it will be your jab at practically the same angle, but not as exaggerated (Note: Fig. #16, #17). Remember, while in the on-guard position you should feel relaxed, but ready like a fully charged battery, using your energy only when necessary.

#12
(to wide)

#13
(to narrow)

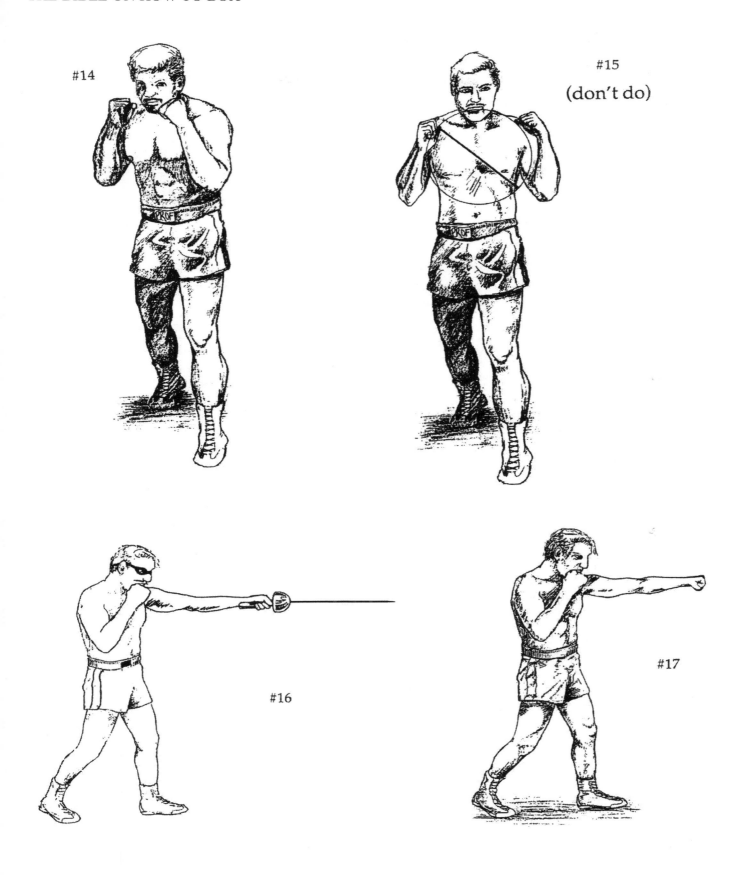

Before we go on to any other lessons, tape or mark off an area to practice **footwork**. About five feet per line and circle it as shown (Note: Fig. #18). Using this circle and two straight lines, you will discover through practice how to form and execute proper footwork. The ideal foot position is one that allows you to move quickly in any direction, for <u>offensive</u> and <u>defensive</u> purposes, by being so balanced as to resist your opponent's punches thrown at you from any angle, using movements to avoid them.

Keeping your right rear heel raised slightly <u>off</u> the floor will allow the back foot easier and quicker movement. The right heel is also raised slightly because when punching weight is transferred to your lead leg, this will be easier if the rear heel is already raised. Also, when you're <u>hit</u>, or if <u>ducking</u> a punch or <u>fading backwards</u> to avoid one, your body has to <u>give</u> a little, sinking down on the <u>rear</u> heel will do this, acting as if it were a "shock absorber" (Note: Fig. #19, #20)

#18

#19

#20

Use this circle pictured below to practice footwork without disturbing your bodies true balance; slide your feet along the floor so that the fundamental position of your body is maintained, this is the key. To take a step forward, lift and pull with your <u>lead</u> leg, your <u>left</u>, keeping your <u>rear leg</u> or <u>right leg</u> on the floor, dragging it as shown (Note: Fig. #21, #22, #23, #24). Keeping your <u>rear</u> leg on the <u>floor</u> while moving <u>forward</u> helps you to maintain your balance with movement and allows you to maintain a foundation to box from.

#21

#22

#23

#24

It's best to take two or three medium steps rather than one or two large steps to cover the same distance (Note: Fig. #25 - #31), this helps you to maintain your balance. Taking too long or large a step could be a costly mistake, it leaves your legs too far apart, therefore negates quick movement, and leaves you momentarily off balance, (Note: Fig. #32 - #33), on what <u>not</u> to do, you need to maintain your body's composure at all times (Note: Fig. #34).

In <u>moving backwards,</u> the same procedure applies, move your lead leg first; in this case the lead leg is your <u>right</u> leg (rear leg). Because this is the direction you want to go towards, lift and pull your right leg, and drag on the floor in front of you your left leg (Note: Fig. #35 - #38). Keeping your left leg on the floor (while moving backwards) helps you to maintain a fighting balance with movement and allows you to maintain a foundation to box from, repeat this until it becomes second nature.

#35

#36

#37

#38

When circling to your right, first pull with your lead leg (your right leg), (the darker foot) and drag behind it on the floor your left leg (the lighter foot). Using footprints may help you to better understand proper footwork (Note: Fig. #39 - #42). Circling to <u>your right</u> nullifies an opponent's right lead, remember you will be moving towards your opponent's left, so carry your right hand a little higher than ordinary when circling or moving towards <u>your right</u>. This is also used to get into position for left hand counters and keeps your opponent off balance. It is imperative that you <u>always, always</u> maintain your on-guard position throughout any movement. (Moving <u>first</u> → → lift and pull the darkest foot. (Moving <u>second</u> → drag, keeping on the floor the <u>lighter</u> foot).

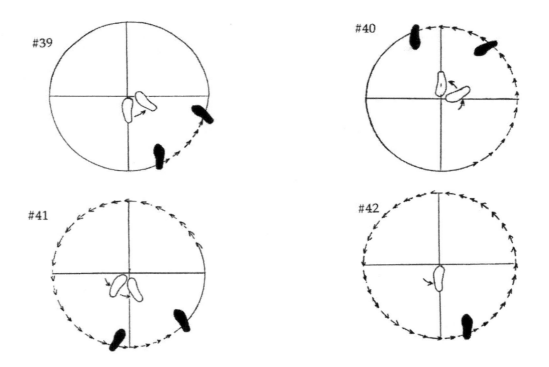

When circling to your left, <u>first</u> lift and pull your lead leg (your left leg), (the darker foot) and drag behind it on the floor, your right leg (the lighter foot) (Note: Fig. #43 - #46). <u>Remember, in whatever direction you are moving, move that leg first</u>. This is very important, if you move the opposite leg first you will be off balance and vulnerable to your opponent's punches. When and if it's necessary to move quickly, take small enough steps so that your center of gravity is rarely out of control, and never cross your legs!

(Note: Fig. #47 Proper Stance). (Note: Fig. #48, #49) on what <u>NOT</u> to do) (Moving <u>first</u> → → lift and pull the <u>darkest</u> foot).

(Moving <u>second</u> → drag, keeping on the floor the <u>lighter</u> foot).

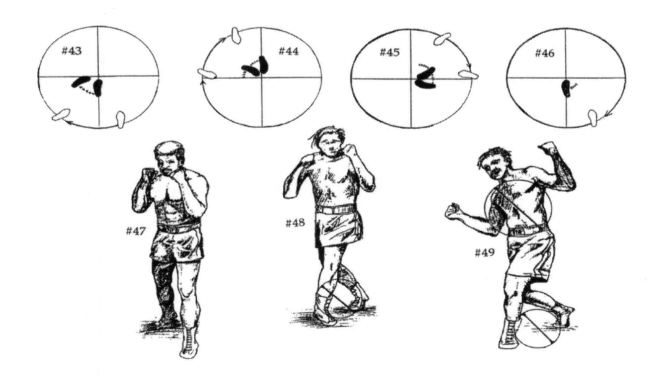

Work on obtaining good balance while in motion. Moving or circling left is also helpful if fighting a southpaw, because you're constantly moving away from his power hand or <u>his left</u> (Note: Fig. #50 - #53). The orthodox fighter's (black trunks) left foot movement creates good positioning for the use of his jab or hook, or in setting up his <u>right hand</u> lead.

Both moving or circling left and right (lateral movement) or back and forth (in and out movement) should be worked on for weeks or months <u>before</u> moving on to <u>any</u> other stages of boxing!

The boxer, who neglects this footwork, is like a professional body builder forgetting to build up the muscles in his legs, as a result, creating an off balance appearance (Note: Fig. #54). In boxing, it's very noticeable if you have no footwork, it means you have no measure of defense or attack, no foundation to work with, nothing to carry you (Note: Fig. #55).

In boxing, you're as good as your footwork allows you to be, so work hard and practice constantly on it. Once the movements become easily performed, add a little speed to the movements and vary the directions. Remember this, if a man is <u>slow</u> on his <u>feet</u>, he will be <u>slow</u> with his <u>punches</u>. Footwork is the foundation of boxing, <u>period</u>!

Chapter 2

BOXERS PUNCHING TOOLS

Keep both feet in a balanced position at all times, hands held in an on-guard position, ready to cover up as well as attack. The <u>first</u> punch to learn is the **<u>jab</u>**. The <u>jab</u> is a straight punch delivered with your lead hand (left hand), also notice when the jab is out, your left shoulder should be protecting your chin from a possible right counter (Note: Fig. #56 - #58).

With the jab, as well as all other punches, your fists are always aimed at penetrating an area, or aimed at punching beyond the selected area (Note: Fig. #59), in essence we punch <u>through</u> an object or an opponent, not just at one.

This punch is completed when the palm is facing downward. Remember, hand is straight (top and side) and we are punching with the top knuckles of the hand, straight out, straight back (Note: Fig. #60 - #64)

#56

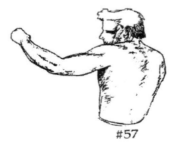

#57

#58

The jab is both an offensive and defensive weapon, as a defensive weapon, the jab will confuse your opponent, off-set his attacks, and frustrate him. Used correctly, it's the sign of a scientific fighter, one who uses strategy instead of force, requiring skill, timing, speed and deception! Practice the jab until it's a light, easy, natural movement. It will take some time before it becomes automatic and has power and speed behind it without any visible effort. Practice and practice until you can deliver a jab with pinpoint accuracy!

The <u>shortest</u> distance between two points is a straight line, therefore making good sense to lead with your jab. The jab is snapped out, not pushed out, and should be brought back exactly the same level it was delivered (Note: Fig. #65 - #69). This should be about shoulder height. The arm merely relaxes and sinks back to the body rather than being pulled back. Do not throw a jab out and drop it, even one inch, on its return to your body, or drop your right while jabbing (Note: Fig. #70 Proper Stance). (Note: Fig. #71 - #74) on what <u>NOT</u> to do; this will definitely invite a counter punch from your opponent.

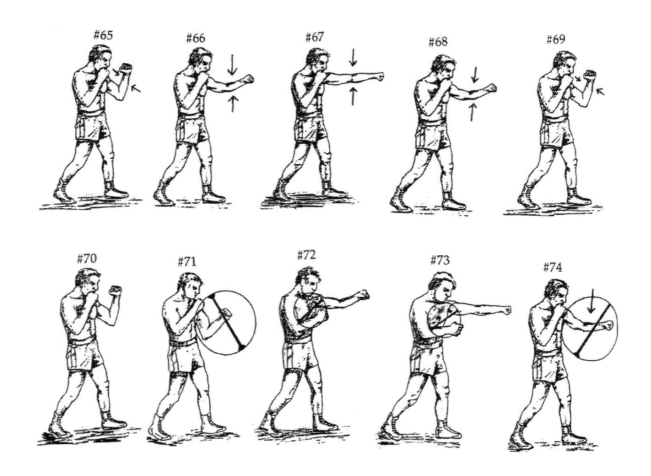

A good jab should be like a cobra striking, quickly and deadly. In offense it keeps your opponent off balance. The jab also <u>sets up</u> all other punches and aggravates your opponent. The jab when used properly can cut and hurt an opponent; I have observed it used to outpoint an opponent in many boxing matches! I've seen a good jab knock down many fighters! The jab is a punch for "all reasons."

Step in when you punch (Note: Fig. #75 - #77), but don't over shoot your target. <u>Over shooting</u> is missing by going too far beyond your intended target. This will leave your opponent in a position to counter, and it may also appear you have no coordination.

Remember, never <u>telegraph a punch</u>. Meaning, never indicate that you are going to throw a particular punch by first pulling back, making face gestures, squinting eyes, or opening your mouth. All or any of these could be judged as telegraphing a punch (Note: Fig #78 - #79), more on this later.

After hitting or after missing your punch, instantly get back to your on-guard position, never lower or drop your other hand while punching, not even an inch (Note: Fig. #80 - #83). Once the jab becomes natural to you, without over-shooting it, telegraphing it, lowering it on its execution or its return, or lowering your right hand while punching with your left, <u>only</u> then it will be time to go on to the next punch.

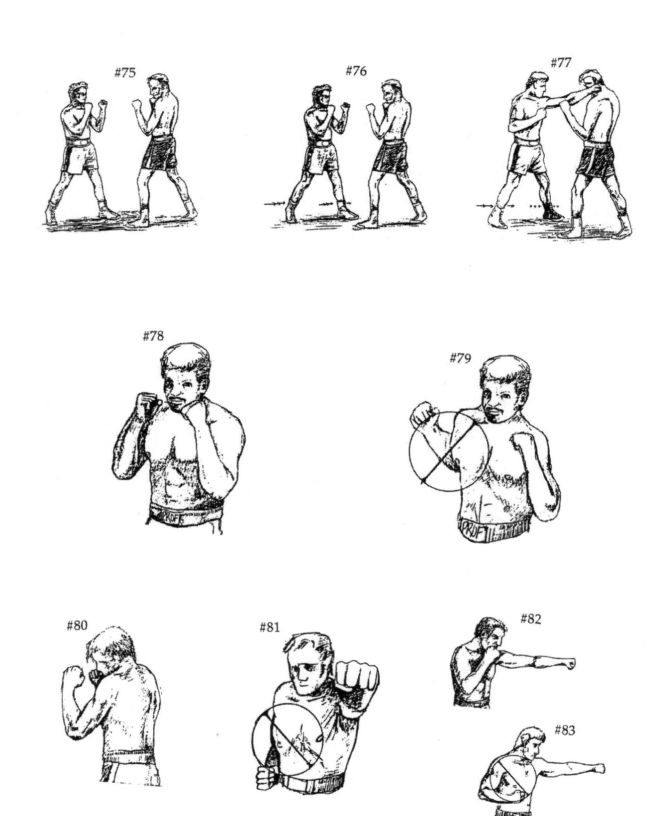

When throwing the **right cross** after a left jab, it has been referred to as the "old one-two." Remember this, "one hand out, one hand back, one hand out, one hand back" (Note: Fig. #84 - #91). As you prepare to deliver your right hand, your left should be already on it's way back to your on-guard position. For defensive reasons, never leave both hands out at any time while punching.

While throwing the straight right, your rear leg <u>pivots</u> on the ball of your rear foot (the right), your <u>hip</u> and <u>torso</u> turn towards the punch; your right shoulder is lifted slightly. Notice how your chin is protected by your right shoulder and is turned in towards your chest slightly (Note: Fig. #92 - #95). On impact, the hand is already tight and palm is facing down, this is a <u>straight right</u>. Remember, the rear <u>heel</u>, the <u>hip</u> and the <u>shoulder</u> all turn at the same time; not one before the other.

Remember, for real power the punch comes from the center of your body, by shifting your body weight as a door hinge would; think of a door slamming! The upper door hinge cannot move before its counterpart, the lower door hinge; they always move together in unison, never independently! (Note: Fig. #96 - #97). Again, punch through your opponent, and hit as straight as possible. When throwing the right cross (straight right) keep the punch close to your body, don't lift your elbow up in the slightest (as if you had a birds wing), that will turn the punch into a hook, hooks are much slower than straight punches, the right hook being the slowest of all.

The straight right is also very effective as a lead punch against a southpaw. It is the most powerful punch an orthodox fighter has when it's thrown correctly. When executed properly, the straight right (right cross) has a tremendous impact on your opponent. Don't forget, the shortest distance between two points is a straight line, so throw your jab and right cross as straight as possible. Thrown <u>after</u> the <u>jab</u> it's referred to as a <u>right cross</u>, when thrown as <u>lead</u> punch or <u>otherwise</u> it's referred to as a <u>straight right</u> but it <u>is</u> the same punch.

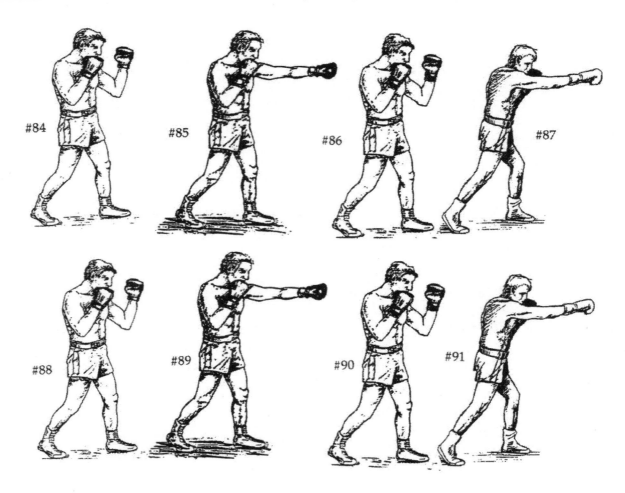

The **left hook** is a punch that comes from the side, usually outside the range of an opponent's vision, as to go around an opponent's guard. This is valuable when in close quarters to your opponent or for body punching after you have hurt your opponent with a straight blow. The left hook, is many a great fighters' best weapon in his arsenal, and is very effective when thrown off or after the left jab, or after the straight right. Hooks like the straight right are punches that have your body weight behind them; making them very powerful blows when delivered properly. Practice this in slow motion, notice how the arm is brought up as if you can place a quarter on your elbow and it would not fall off. The left hook is never a wide looping blow, never a swing, it's more like a tight, close to your body crisp or snappy punch (Note: Fig. #98 - #104). Remember, the pivot is the key!

The left foot now becomes the pivot, your left hip turns as the elbow is bent over (think of that quarter) and the palm of left hand is now facing down, and knuckles are pointed in the direction of your shifting weight. Footwork makes the punch; this punch can't be left out for a split second longer than it has to. If the punch misses or lands, return your arm taking the same path, back to your on-guard position quickly! Also note the line on the boxing trunks, at the start, midway through and at the finish of the left hook; notice how it moved; it's the pivot!

Think of speed, and more speed, drive the blow through your opponent, remember not to open a hook, when this is done it becomes a swing. Swings should **never** be used, they're slow revealing a lack of skill and they lack power; they'll also get you hurt if your opponent counters, and swing type of punches give your opponent much more time to counter! (Note: Fig. #105, #106).

#98 (start)

(midway) #99

(midway) #100

(midway) #101

#102 (finish)

#103 (finish)

(finish) #104

#105

#106

The **<u>right hook</u>** is thrown in the same manner as you would throw the straight right, but your elbow is bent, just like the left hook (Note: Fig. #107 - #111). The right hooks, while fighting in an orthodox position should be used only after other punches have landed and have paved the way for this blow. Remember, this punch comes from your rear hand and is shortened by the bend of the elbow to form the hook. Therefore, it takes much more time to land than the straight right and should be used with caution.

The right hook comes in handy when fighting at close range. When throwing both left hook and right hook punches towards your opponent's body, keep your other hand held a slight bit higher to shield your face, and your elbow in close to your body to protect your ribs, crouching slightly at the waist (Note: Fig. #112, #113).

#108
(midway)

#109
(midway)

(midway) #110

(start) #107

#111 (finish)

#112

#113

<u>Uppercuts</u> are punches primarily used for inside fighting but can be used as an offensive counter blow when timed properly. Throwing an uppercut is somewhat like throwing a hook with the exception of the placement of your arm and hand, shown is the **left uppercut** (Note: Fig. #114 - #118), keeping elbow close to your body, again footwork is essential. Dipping down slightly before unleashing your uppercut will add unseen power to the blow, but this is not always necessary.

The pivot once again is crucial, **never** pull back your arm or hand before throwing, and remember to return to the on-guard position quickly!

(start)
(right side view)
#114

(midway)
(front view)
#115

(midway)
(front view)

(midway)
(front view)
#117

(finish)
(front view)
#118

When throwing the **right uppercut** the same procedure applies, as in <u>all power punches</u>, <u>the pivot</u>. On completion of the punch your palm is facing toward you as if you were doing a bicep curl. Remember the direction of your weight follows your knuckles. Keep elbows close to your body; never reach out to hit your opponent. This punch is to be used close to your body, so you won't be leaving yourself open too long a time for an opponent's counter (Note: Fig. #119 - #123). Uppercuts come in handy when your opponent is crouching down. These blows should straighten him right up! (Note: Fig. #124 - #125).

Chapter 3

* RHYME & REASON *

Believe it or not, there are only **eight punches in boxing**, the jab, right cross, left hook, right hook, left uppercut, right uppercut and from the southpaw stance the right jab and left cross (Note: Fig. #126 - #133).

#126
(jab)

#127
(right cross)

#128
(left hook)

#129
(right hook)

#130
(left upper cut)

#131
(right upper cut)

#132
south-paw
right jab

#133
south-paw
left cross

These eight punches thrown one after the other <u>in any order</u> are called **<u>combinations</u>**. One punch should naturally <u>set up</u> the next in boxing, the same way one shot, should set up the next in a game of pool. Before arriving at this analogy, I have spent many long hours and many years of playing pool with my closest friends. In our early years before acknowledging the true importance of combinations the game was lacking something. Combinations are equally important to the art of boxing! Without them there would be <u>no art</u> in the Art of Boxing, and the sport of boxing wouldn't be! Here's a simple planned combination to help get the point across (Note: Fig. #134, #135).

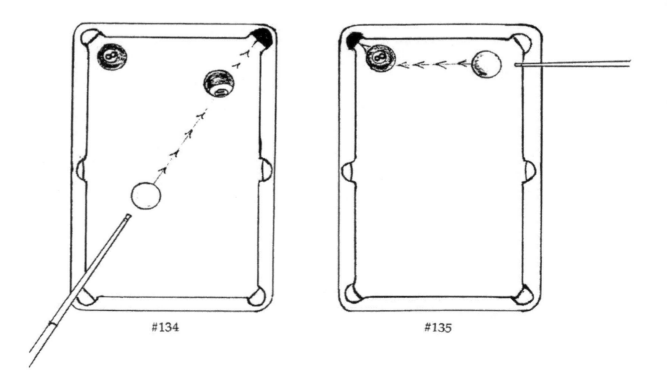

#134   #135

Try throwing your punches using a phrase I conceived for boxing called **"RHYME & REASON."** "Rhyme" meaning, punches in bunches <u>more than one</u>, <u>more than one</u>, punches set in motion without a break in their sequence, thrown in combination using a rhythmic measure. "Reason" meaning, <u>hard</u> definite punches using determination, commitment and great effort thrown with <u>bad intentions</u>, establishing and commanding authority.

When throwing combinations, these punches must be thrown with "Rhyme & Reason" if they're not, they'll lack boldness, certainty, and the firmness of purpose.

When you see an opening in your opponent's guard, caused possibly by a punch he missed or by your doing, you must attack immediately you <u>can't</u> be lackadaisical, especially when throwing combinations.

For instance, let's say your first punch in your combination was thrown with "reason" but your next two or three were thrown flimsy, lazy, or with no substance, no "reason" you can be countered very easily, and hurt badly by your opponent's counter punch. Each and every one of your punches thrown in combination must be thrown with "reason."

The first <u>combination</u> to master, is the jab, right cross, and left hook in this order, thrown to the same area, starting with the level of

#136   #137   #138   #139   #140

your own shoulders (Note: Fig. #136 - #140

When this first combination is worked on and much improvement is seen, add two or three jabs to it, then the right cross and left hook. Then practice double jabbing to the face, right cross to the face and the left hook to the body, bringing your body down to that level, for the left hook to <u>his</u> body, do this by crouching and bending your knees and never forget to pivot on <u>all</u> power punches! The <u>only</u> punches that <u>do not</u> require a pivot are <u>jabs</u>; all other punches <u>are</u> considered power punches! (Note: Fig. #141 - #155).

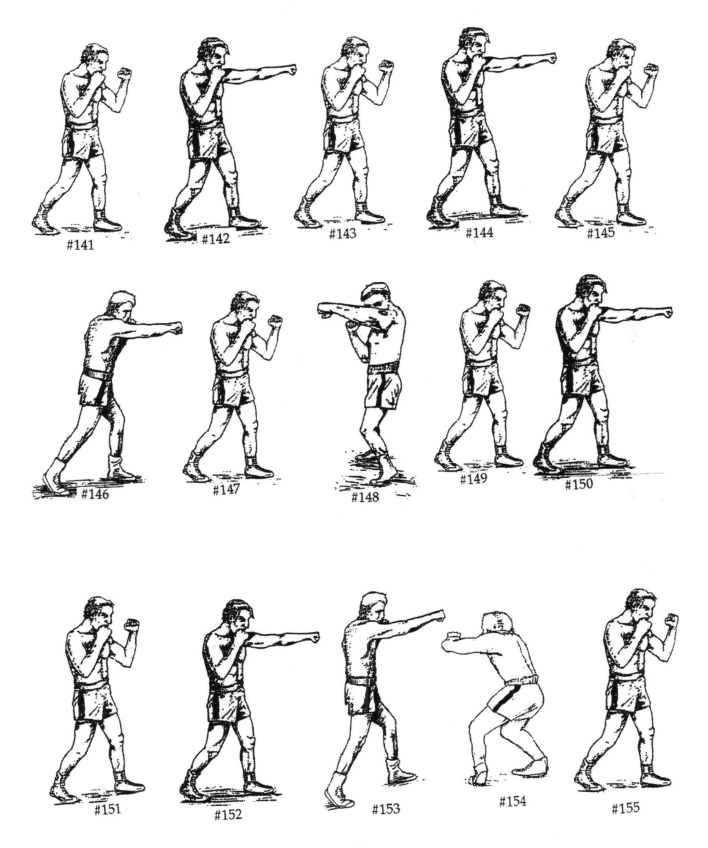

The next combination to work on could go like this; jab, right cross, left hook to the body, right hook to the body, back away and jab to the face (Note: Fig. #156 - #178). The different sequences and the variety of combinations are endless, what's always most important, first and foremost is that you throw all of your punches using <u>correct form</u>, once this is mastered throw all your punches with "reason" and most of your punches in "rhyme."

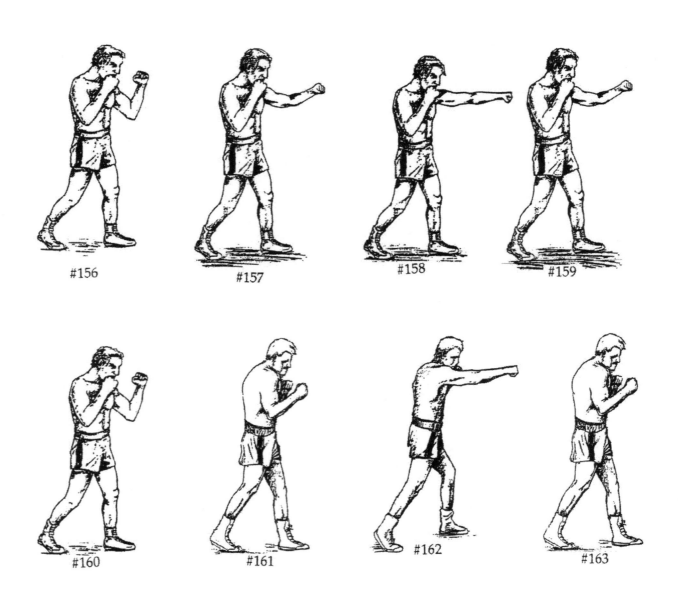

#156   #157   #158   #159

#160   #161   #162   #163

Referring back to the jab, the jab often paves the road for all other punches and there are punches that <u>can</u> be **<u>released off the jab</u>**. For instance, the <u>hook off the jab</u>; first jab, then on its return, turn that punch into a <u>hook</u> by returning it to the point where the hook will begin, and <u>not</u> completely back to the on-guard position (Note: Fig. #179 - #186). Remember to turn your hip and pivot on the ball of the left foot, turn over your hand and roll your shoulder with the punch <u>all in unison</u>. Return in the reverse manner back into your on-guard position. Practice until you develop the movements without any hesitation or awkwardness. The move must be fluid and the punch must be crisp!

We can also release an <u>uppercut off the jab</u>, to do so, first jab and <u>without</u> taking your jab completely back, turn your hand into a hook that's going upward, into an uppercut (Note: Fig. #187 - #193). When throwing an uppercut off the jab, remember <u>not</u> to pull back in the slightest, not even an inch (Note: Fig. #194) on what <u>not</u> to do. Remember to keep your right hand up in readiness of your opponent's left hook counter. Once again the <u>pivot is the key</u>, use your hip and body in bringing the power into the punch, dipping slightly will add even more unseen power into the punch.

Always use caution when turning a jab over into an uppercut, especially if your jab missed its mark. Your opponent may counter with <u>his</u> right cross (Note: Fig. #195, #196), this is why it is essential to be as <u>quick</u> as possible, think speed, and more <u>speed.</u>

53

#194

#195

#196

To throw both the <u>hook</u> and <u>uppercut</u> off the <u>same jab</u>, use the same procedure in the hook off the jab, then without bringing your jab back to the on-guard position after the hook pivot, you must then, re-pivot for the uppercut (Note: Fig. #197 - #207). Again, jab, hook with pivot, arm back most of the way to the point where the uppercut should begin and re-pivot while throwing uppercut as shown, turning your punch upward. Practice this combination until it becomes smooth, with speed and power behind it. This is an **advanced combination**, and should be perfected <u>before</u> using it in an actual bout.

#202

#203

#204

#205

#206

#207

To successfully throw **(Body Punches)** <u>punches towards</u> your <u>opponent's body</u>, **first you must lower your body to the level of that particular area you wish to strike.** This is to say, the lower your punch, the lower your body in conjunction to that punch. To accomplish this, you have to bend your knees and slightly bend at the waist, always maintaining the on-guard position <u>before</u> and <u>after</u> each punch. Never throw a punch targeted towards your opponent's body from an <u>upright position</u> (Note: Fig. #208), this will lessen the power of the blow and leave you wide open for counter punches.

When delivering any body punches, remember the same principles apply as if you were delivering head blows. While in on-guard position, pivot when throwing hooks, uppercuts and rear hand punches. Remember don't telegraph punches (refer to Chapter 4). Hands are **never pulled back** or lowered when withdrawing (Note: Fig. #209). Remember not to drop or lower any punch without <u>first lowering your bodies position</u> (Note: Fig: #210).

Punch and return back to your on-guard position or into a combination of punches, as with all punches, get into a habit of returning along the <u>same</u> path used when starting the punch. Many times the opponent's body is the easier target. The body covers a far larger surface than the chin. The body is less mobile, and you have about one foot of body to aim at, for every inch of chin. Landing a solid punch to your opponent's solar plexus could render him completely helpless, yes, with only one punch!

Good body punching is a sign of maturity in a fighter, "kill the body and the head will die," goes the old saying. It's good to jab or feint first to get your distance and leverage when throwing body punches. We will get into feints later. Always vary your punches high/low, low/high, learn to be a versatile fighter, keeping your opponent guessing! (Note: Fig. #211 - #220).

In-fighting is simply fighting at close range, getting inside. While in-fighting it's necessary to bob and weave, slip punches, draw and feint, and at times just simply muscle yourself in close to your opponent and bang away, we will soon cover all of this in Chapter 4. Inside fighting is more suited for the slugger, brawler, the heavy hitter and/or the slower man, but can also be used successfully by the boxer/puncher on a limited basis!

Chapter 4

BOXERS TOOLS OF MOVEMENT

Have you ever heard the phrase "It's not how fast it travels, but how soon it gets there that counts?" Remember **speed** and **timing** complement each other. Speed in delivering a punch will lose most of its effectiveness or its target completely, unless the punch is properly timed. A good boxer faced with equal opposition, at times must sense, rather than preconceive his chance to punch, "timing a punch along with its proper execution is the true secret of powerful hitting."

Remember this, the more powerful boxer need <u>not</u> be the stronger of the two, but the one that can exert his strength <u>quickly</u>, since **power equals force times speed**. If the boxer throws faster punches he increases his power. For example, take a smaller lighter man swinging a <u>baseball bat</u>, he may hit the ball harder, faster and farther than the heavier bigger man who swings just a bit slower.

Another example, when I was 15 years old and weighed about 140lbs., there was this punch machine at the arcade, it was a speed bag with a power gauge of some kind. When striking the bag the gauge would display how hard it was hit. I would make the gauge go around completely, ring a bell and sometimes go around twice with one punch (my straight right).

I would then observe other men who weighed 200lbs. or more, of solid muscle, hit the bag and make the gauge go <u>less</u> than half way around (Note: Fig. #221, #222). Remember, the <u>speed</u> of your hands thrown using <u>proper form</u>, determines the degree of <u>power</u> in your punches. Another example: take a bowling ball, and throw it at a wall, alright now take that same bowling ball and shoot it out of a cannon, get the picture! (Note: Fig. #223 - #224). Utilizing speed with the proper form, your punches will be felt before they're seen! This reminds me of the Roy Jones Jr. vs. Vinny Pazienza fight on June 24, 1995. The hand and foot speed of Roy was just too much for Vinny to handle. Vinny simply could not get into range to punch the quicker more elusive Roy Jones Jr. Simply, power equals force times <u>speed</u>! Roy's punches were felt before they were seen.

Feinting can require using the eyes, hands, shoulders, legs or the whole body in a single effort to deceive your opponent, making a move or gesture that you are going to do one thing, or throw a certain punch and do another thing, or throw a different punch (Note: Fig. #225 - #227). These movements are really lies or decoys and as your opponent attempts to adjust his defense, the skilled boxer takes advantage of the openings created. If your opponent blinks when you feint, use your opponent's split second of blindness to launch your attack, leave him in the dark (Note: Fig. #228 - #230). Feinting can be used to lure your opponent into a trap, and if he takes the bait he will be playing into your hand!

Feinting is also used to determine what the opponent's reaction will be to each movement you make. Remember, feinting creates only momentary openings. To be able to take advantage of these openings, means instant reflex action or before knowledge of what openings will be created by certain feints. Only through actual practicing of many feints against different styles and kinds of opponents, may a general reaction tendency be determined. A good fighter will know openings; will result by feinting, therefore testing his opponent's readiness and defensive moves and making use of this new found knowledge by initiating his follow-up action almost before the opening occurs. Feints used too often in the same manner will enable the opponent to time them for his counter attack, thus defeating their purpose. So when feinting, mix them up, or change their pace. Don't rely on them solely. For any feint to work, you must master the boxing fundamentals and all possible counters for each punch.

Telegraphing is like mailing your opponent a post card, telling him what punch you will throw next, or sticking a note on your forehead saying, "now I will throw a right", alright now I will throw a left and so on. This is usually done by pulling back on your punch before executing it, or dropping your arm before throwing it, even the slightest amount will be telling your opponent of your next move or punch. Squinting your eyes, or making a certain face gesture before punching, if constant, all can be used against you!

A good trainer or boxer will pick up on the slightest fault you have in order to gain victory over you (Note: Fig. #231). Don't <u>telegraph</u> your punches, if you find you are, go back to the basics & fundamentals; you may be trying too hard. When you punch you need to use leverage from proper foot placement and fluid movement in your punches. All punches are thrown from where your hand is at <u>that</u> <u>moment</u> of the opening, or the moment the punch starts, <u>without</u> pulling back first, or repositioning! **Starting a punch is a forward movement!! I cannot overemphasize that!**

<u>Drawing</u> is closely related to feinting, where as in feinting an opening is created, in drawing some part of the body is left <u>unprotected</u> <u>purposely</u>. So a particular blow may be led by your opponent, developing opportunities for you to counter his punches. Drawing is usually practiced by the quicker of the two men, or woman by leaving a spot unprotected purposely and knowing the available or probable punch his opponent will try, is more than ready to counter punch, having confidence in his ability to out speed his challenger (Note: Fig. #232 - #235).

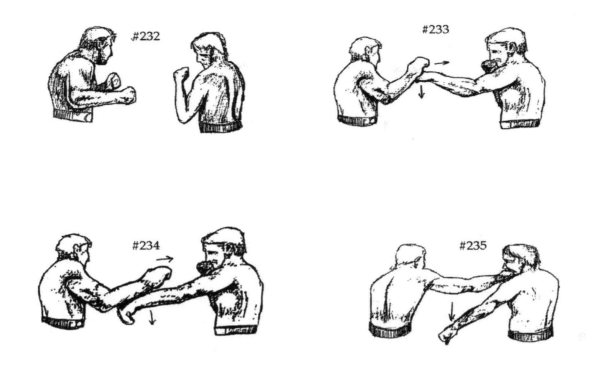

Ducking, is a defensive move, ducking is used to avoid a punch directed at your head. It's a movement using the on-guard position. Keeping arms in slightly closer to your body and bending at the waist and knees in a single effort to avoid a punch. In order to be successful at this, the move must be <u>late</u> and <u>quick</u>. Ducking can also be used in an offensive manner, as in a counter. For instance, after ducking the punch, keeping balance and poise, on your way up deliver one or more of your own punches, uppercuts or hooks when thrown out of a crouch have more power behind them if thrown correctly, using your body and an extra push from your legs (Note: Fig. #236 - #241).

<u>Slipping</u>, is a defensive move, a quick movement of your body or head to one side, it's used to avoid your opponent's punches. Remember to move late, but quick, and only far enough to avoid the punch by the tiniest of margins. Do not try to make your opponent miss by a mile. Remember this, "any miss is as good as a mile." It's very important to keep your balance <u>while</u> in motion using range as a protective device, making that slight movement, late and quick, allows you to keep a clear view of your opponent at all times. Enabling you to counter when the precise moment occurs. To slip hooks, swerve your head backwards (fading back) slightly enough to just miss, or move in, causing the punch to go behind your head, depending on your fighting style (Note: Fig. #242, #243).

With any offensive or defense move, <u>never</u> take your eyes off your opponent. You might be asking yourself, how will I know how far to move when slipping punches? The answer is, you will in time, through proper training and practice. To slip straight punches, move your head to one side, preferably the side that will allow you the best position for counter punches. There's the <u>inside slip</u>, use this to end up on the inside of your opponent's punch. There's also the <u>outside slip</u>, a safer move, moving to the outside of your opponent's punch. (Note: Fig. #244, #245).

If avoiding the punch completely is not possible, <u>parrying</u> the punch is the answer.

#242 (fading back).

#243 (move in)

#244   (inside slip)

#245 (outside slip)

Parrying is a defensive move, it's a block, a quick short movement using your open right hand (Note: Fig. #246). Your hand should come in contact with your opponent's punch in order to deflect it from its original path. The parry is a light easy movement, depending on timing not force. Never reach out to parry a punch. Always wait until it's very close to you, reaching out to meet it may enable your opponent to change the direction of his punch, or you may create an opening in your defense by doing so, giving your opponent that slight opening he may be waiting for. Remember parry late, not early, this way your opponent is not able to read your response, especially if he is feinting.

(parry)
#246

Blocking punches thrown to the sides of your body <u>can</u> be blocked by using your elbows, simply lower your arm and crouch slightly to that side. (Note: Fig. #247). The elbows along with your arms, shoulders or hands can and should block your opponent's punches taken they are aimed toward that particular area. Never bring your arms out to meet a punch, just move your arm into your body protecting the targeted area, tightening your stomach and arm muscles in an effort to absorb the punch, and move, or punch back, but never attempt "rope a dope" don't stay there and absorb punishment. Taking punches as if <u>you</u> were a heavy bag, will transform <u>you</u> into becoming one, you'll just start to hang around with not much to say! There's no reason to attend the "school of hard knocks". If you're getting hit too often, <u>move</u> or go down to one knee and take an eight count from the referee, clear your head! Taking too many punches will leave you intoxicated with punches, a.k.a "<u>punch-drunk</u>" (Note: Fig. #248).

#247

#248

Bobbing is somewhat like ducking, it's movement <u>up</u> and <u>down</u> used to avoid punches and can be used to confuse your opponent (Note: Fig. #249 - #251). **Weaving** is a <u>side</u> <u>to</u> <u>side</u> movement, also used to avoid punches and to keep your opponent guessing your next move (Note: Fig. #252 - #253). When used together, <u>bobbing</u> <u>and</u> <u>weaving</u> can be extremely useful for defensive purposes as well as offensive purposes. Here's one way to practice bobbing and weaving (Note: Fig. #254 - #256).

Remember to keep hands up to guard your face, and elbows close to your body to guard your sides. Keeping chin down and into your chest slightly. Eyes forward watching your opponent's every move, <u>not</u> watching the floor or your opponent's feet but watch either his <u>chest</u> or <u>eyes</u>. By doing this, you can see all that's happening.

Never, at any time during a bout should you look anywhere else other than at your opponent, <u>defending yourself at all times</u>!

Even if the boxing referee interferes or delays the bout, still keep one eye on your opponent. Remember you are in a real fight; it's not a Disney ride or fake world wrestling entertainment.

#249   (bobbing)   #250   (bobbing)   #251

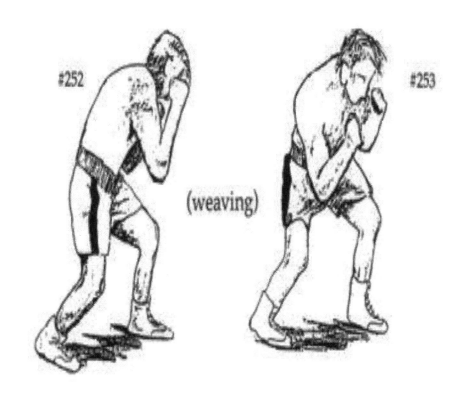

#252   (weaving)   #253

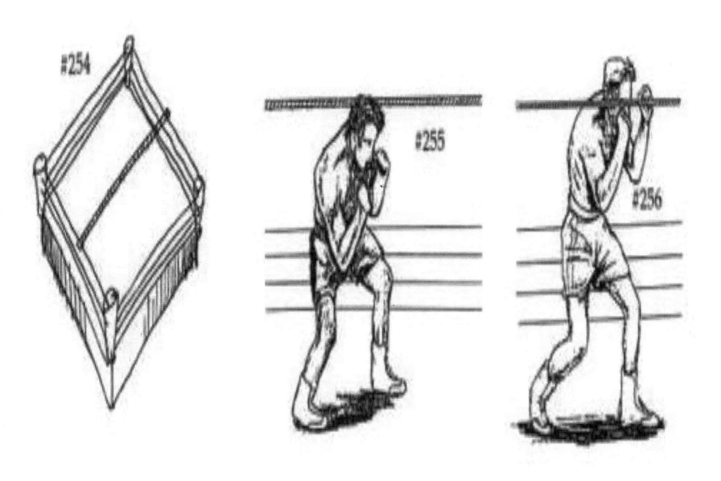

Sidestepping properly used, is not only one of the prettiest moves, but it's also a method of escaping all kinds of attacks, and in turn countering an opponent when he least expects it. The art of sidestepping, as of art of ducking and slipping, is to move late and quick, you wait until your opponent's punch is almost on you, and then take a quick step, either to the right or left (Note: Fig. #257 - #259).

This puts you in a different position, or angle, to counter his punch, taking advantage of this new position and whatever openings there may be, sidestepping can also be used offensively and defensively.

#257   #258   #259

Chapter 5

* *THE BOXING WORKOUT* *

First, we must practice long and hard on what we have learned up to now, before attempting any sparring or bag hitting. The reason being, if someone starts hitting bags or sparring partners before learning and mastering most of the basic fundamentals, he would in no doubt start picking up bad habits and perfecting them. Hitting the bag incorrectly can also injure your hands. Sparring too soon, even supervised can injure much more. So, let's take our time when learning, to be safe, gain confidence and to avoid injury.

What we will now do is practice what is called **shadow boxing**. Shadow boxing can be practiced in the ring or in front of a large mirror (Note: Fig. #260, #261). Shadow boxing is like going through Katas, Forms or Patterns used in the martial arts. Shadow boxing is an exercise using the actual boxing movements and punches required in a bout. It's a practice run of what we have already learned, performed as if there were an actual opponent in front of you. Try to imagine an opponent throwing punches at you and you avoiding his and countering with your own punches. Use every move you have learned from this book. Shadow boxing will help you to become strong, confident and secure in your balance and movements. What this training will also do is develop your skills and coordination. Each movement performed strengthens the connections involved and makes the next movement easier and more certain.

Likewise, the lack of use, or <u>after a layoff in training</u>, tends to weaken any pathways that may have formed and makes that movement more difficult and uncertain. When beginning or after a layoff period or time of inactivity, <u>start</u> <u>slowly</u>. Don't cram too much into any one day's workout. Remember, don't practice skilled movements once you are fatigued, and practice them only when fresh. Wrong movements tend to happen unexpectedly and if practiced, progress is set back or injury may occur. When fatigued, changeover to exercises that will require less skilled moves, to exercises that will require more stamina or endurance.

#260   #261

What I would like to show you is the best way for <u>you</u> to train, but I don't personally know you. I can only offer you certain stereotype training techniques for the simple reason that training on any level must be adapted to suit the needs of that particular individual. What's important is the way you approach your workouts, approach them with an "I want to" attitude. In this way you will be reminding yourself of all the positive values your efforts will produce, for instance, your increased endurance, increased strength, improved boxing skills, your self-esteem, your appearance, the ability to think and act quick on your feet.

Likewise, if you approach your workouts with the attitude, "I have to" or "I should" in doing this you set yourself up for failure. Your workouts will become boring and unproductive, because of the pressure you're putting on yourself, to simply get through them. If I were to write books on working out to become a boxing world champion, I could fill a book shelf and only touch the surface on how to train.

What I will do is suggest, here are some of my suggestions. <u>First</u>, before any type of exercise or workout, loosen up by **warming up** to the point where perspiration begins, in an effort to prepare your muscles for activity. Warming up will also aid in your performance and help prevent injuries.

Some of your warm-up exercises should include but are not limited to, jumping jacks, running in place, exercise bike, waist movements, circular arm movements, shoulder movements, wrist and ankle movements, neck and jaw movements etc. etc.

Once your body temperature is increased slightly and you begin to sweat, your muscles are warm and pliable; at that point your muscles are ready to be stretched. Remember a <u>cold</u> <u>muscle</u>, is like a cold rubber band, it's <u>not</u> ready to be stretched!

There are many different types of stretches, whichever ones you choose, do them in a slow and sustained manner and avoid any bouncing or jerking movements. Stretch until you feel mild tension in the muscle, relax and hold the stretch for about 7-10 seconds. Stretching will increase your range of motion in all your movements. Your total warm-up for a workout, including your stretching should take about 5-10 minutes, but it's better to warm up and stretch too much rather than too little. Stretching is also a good way to <u>cool</u> <u>down</u> and relax <u>after</u> your workout!

Your <u>hands should be wrapped properly</u> before any bag hitting, using a pair of two inch boxing hand wraps. I use wraps that are 2" by 170" going around my wrist three times, first to get a good foundation (Note: Fig: #262), always overlapping. Then I come down towards my knuckles and wrap them over three times (Note: Fig. #263), leaving my fingers of that hand slightly spread, so when I close my hand the wraps will not be tight, cutting off my blood circulation. Then moving up toward my palm-going around it two times (Note: Fig. #264) and coming back around over my thumb (Note: Fig. #265), back around my palm two times (Note: Fig. #266), then over my thumb on the other side (Note: Fig. #267), and back to the wrist one time around (Note: Fig. #268) working back towards my palm to my knuckles, (Note: Fig. #269) one more time around my knuckles, (Note: Fig. #270) now working it back up to my wrist-around once should do it (Note: Fig. #271). Now either tie it or like my wraps fasten the Velcro.

It is best to rip small pieces of white adhesive tape about 5 inches long pinching the center first, and placing each piece in between each finger excluding the thumbs (Note: Fig. #272). This helps give farther support, and the tape will help to keep the wraps on. The hand wraps are not enough protection for your knuckles, that's why bag gloves are used.

Hand wraps are primarily for protection of the wrist and hand helping to keep them as one, aiding in or preventing any bending of the wrist and protecting the eight bones in the wrist and the nineteen bones in each hand. (Note: Fig. #273).

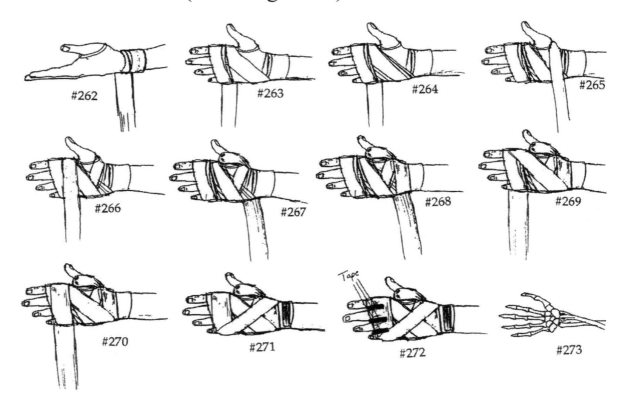

Armed, with a good pair of heavy bag gloves (Note: Fig. #274), and once warmed up, we will start hitting the **heavy bag**. This is used to develop punching power through leverage, by correct foot placement and torso movement. This develops the muscles used in punching, and is the only "opponent" that won't hit back! The bag should be hung so that the bottom of it is about level with <u>your</u> hips. For beginners, start with a 50 lbs. bag. Remember when hitting anything, the <u>hand</u>, <u>wrist</u> and <u>forearm</u> <u>are</u> <u>as</u> <u>one</u>. There is <u>no</u>

bending at the wrist, all the bending is at the elbow. Don't forget to tighten hand <u>before</u> impact, landing all four knuckles squarely, **punching <u>through</u> the bag, <u>not</u> just at it** (Note: Fig. #275).

Heavy bag hitting also makes it possible for you to gauge distances accurately. Practicing to determine how far you are from your opponent is <u>crucial</u> in successfully landing <u>any</u> punches. Here's one example, I had a punching pad taped to a pole in the center of my garage (Note: Fig. #276). This pole supported the second floor and was very sturdy, of this I am sure, because I built that house myself. When I punched this <u>pad</u> that was taped on that pole, being too close to it, the power behind the punch was limited, almost smothered (Note: Fig. #277). When I threw the punch too far from the pad on the pole, I missed it or lightly touched it, also ineffective (Note: Fig.#278). But, when my body position was correct the

punch landed with great power and rocked the whole house!! (Note: Fig. #279).

Begin punching the heavy bag, using what I refer as, "the three basic punches" the <u>jab</u>, <u>right</u> <u>cross</u>, and <u>left</u> <u>hook</u> (Note: Fig. #280 - #282). Don't put all of your power and weight into your punches yet. It's far more important to use the <u>correct</u> <u>form</u>, and practice this while hitting the bag. Always check your form, making certain your punches are thrown in the correct manner. I cannot over emphasize this enough, bad habits are easier to learn and master than good ones are! Take it slow; if possible have a mirror next to you, or a <u>knowledgeable</u> and <u>competent</u> trainer, to check your form.

Throw all punches out from your on-guard position and return rapidly back to it. When looking for faults, you're looking for the dropping of either hand (even the slightest amount), either on the execution of the punch or on its return. All punches should be thrown to the <u>level of the release of the punch</u>, meaning, if you throw a punch from a crouching position, it should not land on your opponents forehead if he is standing in an upright position! On what <u>NOT</u> to do; Note: Fig. #283 (a.) front view & (b.) side view. When you are throwing a punch from an upright position, it shouldn't arrive at your opponent's waistline, unless your body is also at that level, also on what <u>not</u> to do (Note: Fig. #284).

Both punches executed in this manner expose too much of a target for your opponent, and that is a big mistake!

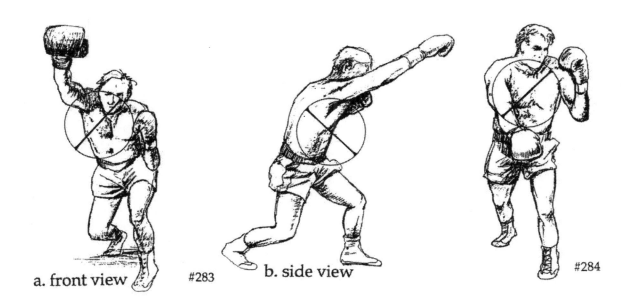

a. front view   #283   b. side view   #284

Always use the right body placement, be sure your hips are used correctly in all power punches. Make certain feet are well balanced in movement as well as when punches are thrown. One hand out, one hand back!

When preparing to launch power punches visualize them being delivered so correctly, they break the heavy bag in two! (Note: Fig. #285). Bring your power up from the balls of your feet, turning your

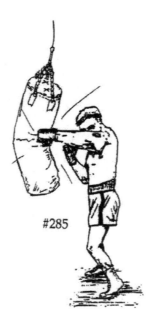

#285

hip and torso, through your shoulders, down your arm focusing that power in your fist, and deliver it through the bag, together in perfect agreement!

Control the bag, the way you would like to control your opponent. Move and punch according to your style. If you're a boxer, jab, double jab and triple jab as you circle in the direction of your jabbing hand. Step in with crisp combinations off the jab, then step out and circle again reversing your movement!

If you're an in-fighter, go in behind your jab and throw head and body combinations. Be versatile and <u>mix-up</u> your combinations, <u>punch</u> don't push. When you become more acquainted with heavy bag hitting, and you are certain your punches are thrown correctly, go on to a heavier bag, one weighing 75 lbs. When you are even more experienced, move up to one weighing 100 lbs. or more, this will improve your punching power. But remember, throwing power punches and using heavier bags also increases your risk of hand injury (Note: Fig. #286) on what NOT to do. Make certain your hands are wrapped properly, and they're tight <u>right</u> before contact and visualize your <u>hand</u> and <u>wrist</u> as one <u>solid</u> <u>straight</u> <u>pipe</u> (Note: Fig. #287). Any type of injury can set you back days, weeks, months or even years.

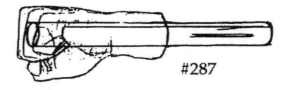

The **double-end bag** (Note: Fig. #288) will help to improve your timing and be an asset to your training, this bag when hit will come back at you quickly, you could imagine it being your opponent's head or body and strike it back repeatedly, or imagine it being your opponent's punch and slip, sidestep, bob and weave or even parry it and counter punch. The double-end bag can be used offensively or defensively, as if it were a willing sparring partner, practice often on it, and make good use of its benefits (Note: Fig. #289).

double-end bag

#288

#289

When using the **speed bag**, make certain the speed bags bottom is slightly higher than your own chins level (Note: Fig. #290). When experienced, this bag can be hit without the use of bag gloves, but hand wraps should be worn. While instructing new boxers to hit the speed bag, I have them slap in instead of punch it, until the movement becomes natural. After slapping it, let the bag come back two or more times at first, until you gain experience with it. The larger bags are the slower ones, start with them first, working towards the smallest and fastest speed bag called the peanut bag.

When you're ready to hit the bag with closed fists, let the bag hit each side of the platform, then hit it again as it comes back (Note: Fig. #291 a-f). This particular exercise will help strengthen your shoulders, if you can keep both hands up throughout each three minute exercise or round. In time, through practice, you will be able to punch the bag quicker, fancier and it will soon become a rhythmic movement.

To prove to you that timing and speed complement each other, try taking half of the bags air out, now hit the speed bag as before, notice how your hand is there, before the bag is back. Hitting your opponent before and after he is there does nothing, but leaves yourself open for his attack; you must land your punches while your opponent is there!!

While punching the **speed bag** using the side of your hand, (Note: Fig. #292) this type of punch is <u>not</u> used in boxing, try not to over develop that movement or bring it into the ring. The speed bag in the beginning is best used to practice the jab, the right cross and left hook. Try not to hit the platform while punching, be careful, take your time, and learn everything properly the first time!

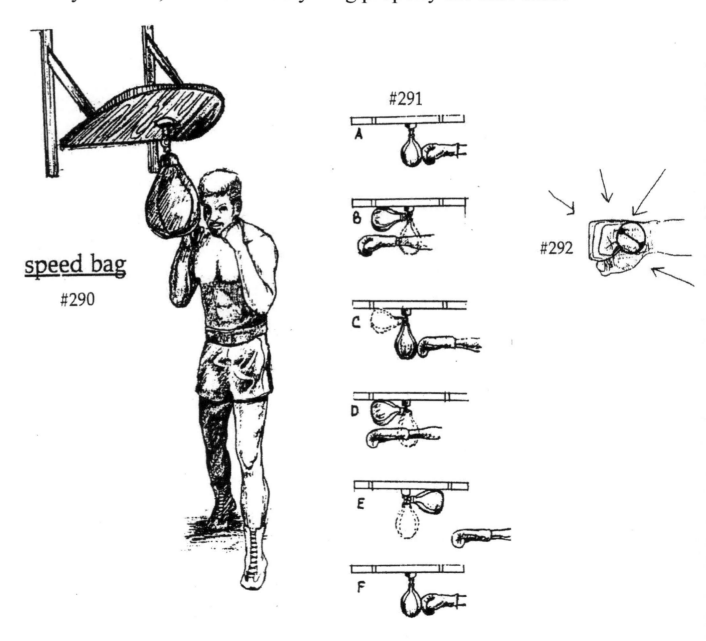

speed bag
#290

#291

#292

There is only one way to eat an elephant "<u>one bite at a time</u>." To become a champion, takes <u>one punch at a time</u>. It would be futile to scuba dive before learning to swim, to run before learning to walk, so it is with boxing, **you must first learn the basics, the fundamentals before any actual sparring or fighting!**

<u>Jumping rope</u> will improve your footwork, cardiovascular efficiency and coordination. While jumping rope has recently been discovered, as an excellent total body exercise in its own right, rope jumping has always been a part of the boxer's workout. Take your time, as with the start of speed bag punching, rope jumping may also be awkward at first. Keep working out with the jump rope, soon you will find your footwork, and coordination improving greatly. At first it will seem difficult, slow or even foolish, but I rate this exercise number two, right behind running, as the best all-around exercise (Note: Fig. #293).

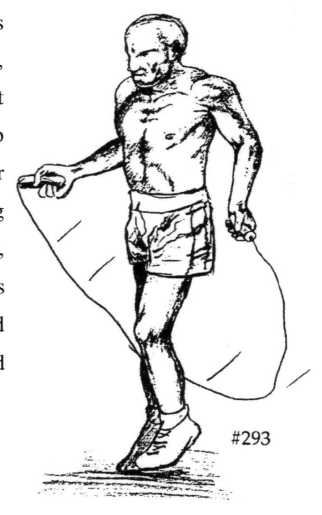

#293

Chapter 6

SPARRING

The basic key to fighting is to take advantage of your opponent's weaknesses, but to detect those weaknesses takes experience, sparring is where you will get it. I remember one instance when I was teaching two close friends of mine Richie and Jimmy the art of boxing. I made the mistake of allowing them to spar too soon. Jimmy at the time was more along with boxing, heavier, older but not yet disciplined, he hit Richie in the stomach so hard I thought Richie would never put on the gloves again.

As it turned out that was the last time they sparred, but both turned out years later to be excellent knowledgeable fighters with power house punches, and Richie's stomach has toughened up since then. Here's another example, I have a close friend from my high school days, and at that time he was on the wrestling team, but wanted to learn to box. I showed him a few things for a day or so, and then I brought him to my trainer at the gym. He had him in the ring sparring within 10 minutes. My friend was so frustrated by getting hit as often as he was, he pulled off his gloves and picked his **sparring** opponent up over his head and was ready to throw him out of the ring! Fortunately with a lot of yelling from me and my trainer, he let him down softly inside the ring. The point is that better trainers <u>never</u> allow <u>any</u> fighters into the ring, to spar, too soon!

The trainer should work with his student slowly, only after months of floor work does he let a fighter begin to spar. Both <u>you</u> and your <u>trainer</u> should feel completely ready and comfortable with the start of your sparring, and with <u>each</u> sparring partner you go in there with (<u>refer to Chapter 8</u>). Remember, sparring fighters heavier than yourself only helps the bigger or heavier man, the lighter fighter may move quicker forcing the heavier fighter to move and keep up with him, but why subject yourself to harder punches than necessary (Note: Fig. #294) spar fighters in your own weight class give or take 8 pounds.

Sparring is a full practice run, and sort of dress rehearsal for the real thing. Sparring is the combat zone for learning and practicing the required skills. Each sparring session is unique and should aid you in your endurance and abilities. Sparring sessions should also sharpen your reflexes until they become instantaneous, lacking any hesitation, spontaneously reacting to your opponent's actions. Sparring will also increase your total boxing knowledge and comprehension through hands on experience. This is where you will actually practice on someone else, while he's practicing on you. Start off slowly on someone you may <u>know</u> and <u>trust</u>. Someone that is more experienced than you and will help you learn, <u>without</u>

beating your head in. Spar only under professional supervision using proper head gear, mouth piece, protective cup, hand wraps, training gloves, sneakers or boxing shoes (Note: Fig. #295).

The first punch to work on, and learn to counter is the jab. Remember, to throw punches much slower at first, to get acquainted with all boxing counters and moves. Have your sparring partner throw his left jab toward your face and you parry it with your open right glove (Note: Fig. #296, #297). Practice that move for a while, when that comes easy, add a right counter off your parry. Do this, by going over your sparring partners left instantly after your parry with <u>your</u> straight right, have his jab glide off your parry deflecting his jab and countering with your right (Note: Fig. #298, #299).

Have your sparring partner throw his jab, you parry it and counter with <u>your</u> left jab (Note: Fig. #300, #301) practice this for a while, once you have these counters mastered, try hooking off the jab after your parry (Note: Fig. #302 - #304). Practice these counters each time you spar, and reverse the roles with your sparring partner. The blocks and counters must become automatic, when they do, add speed and power to the punches, but only when you're both ready and under the watchful eye of your trainer.

I remember when I was younger; I worked as a milkman's helper. I delivered milk door to door from 11:30 pm to 7:30 am in N.Y.C., the milkman's name was Charlie and he became a close friend to me. Charlie a Christian who knew the Bible and used it often, answering questions I had pertaining to life, he also spoke often of the <u>Lord,</u> (*Refer to closing page*) and unknowingly honed my reflexes. Many times during the night he would send me into dark, dark alleys and old run-down buildings for me to find and place the milk in the milk box. There were times I was terrified to do so, but did it anyway, only to find at the end of the darkest alleys or doorway, Charlie quietly and secretly waiting to say, "BOO!" and scare the Hell out of me. All the while this was sharpening my reflexes! I would jump into a fighting stance, in place of running away. I was always a slow runner, that's why I learned how to fight.

Whatever job or occupation that you may have, you can always find ways of turning your mundane lives into small beneficial workouts, or as I did, turn a negative action into a positive reaction! With all your sparring and boxing training, don't let your mental demands exceed your physical capabilities.

Take your time! Don't try too hard too soon! Don't overthrow or over exert! Just relax and keep practicing! Remember, how to eat that elephant! (Note: Fig. #305).

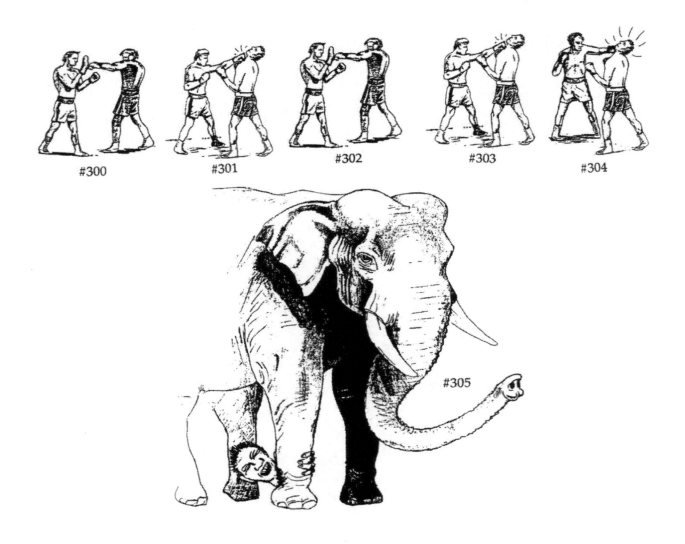

#300   #301   #302   #303   #304

#305

Chapter 7

* FIGHTING STYLES & MY ADVISE *

There are two types of **fighters, <u>mechanical</u> and <u>intellectual</u>**. A mechanical fighter is one who was taught the manner in which punches should be thrown and more than likely can demonstrate them to anyone (Note: Fig. #306). The intellectual fighter has learned the punches in the correct manner also, but takes it one step further, he knows when to use each punch, at a time where it will do him the most good (Note: Fig. #307) and can change the pace, the cadence or the tempo he uses to deliver each punch, in a way that will confuse most mechanical fighters. The intellectual fighter also makes fewer needless motions and more skilled and properly timed moves; this saves energy per movement!

#306

#307

Give all you have, all the time, slips, ducks, bobbing and weaving, they can all be used as an aggressive <u>defense</u> and <u>offense</u> without moving the body out of range. Use range as a protective device by the smallest of margins. <u>Sometimes</u> a good offense is your best defense. A good offensive consists of leads, feints and forward movement, be versatile. Beating your opponent to the punch with lightning fast leads and drawing out your opponents counter punches with feints, in such a way as to make his counter punches miss. Your opponent's miss leaves him out of position and an easy target for a counter punch from you! Always jab as straight as possible. Step in when you punch, punches thrown straight out, should be brought straight back. Don't telegraph any punches, don't overshoot your target. Remember, after hitting or missing, instantly return to your on-guard position. Try starting and finishing all combinations with a <u>jab</u>, using it as a **<u>reset</u>** <u>button</u>, this will help on defense, as well as your set up tool for offense! (Note: Fig. #308), and if openings are still there continue right into another series of punches or combinations!

#308

When fighting in close, the hooks, uppercuts, and body punches are mostly used. Remember, harder punches are delivered from a solid foundation. Lighter punches are delivered from a boxer on his toes. What's needed most times is a combination of both! Don't waste energy or punches; wait until he is within range before attempting any attacks. If your opponent is doing the leading, avoid his punches and hit back with counter punches, before he can get away. Whenever your opponent gets set to punch, move. You will in time develop speed with the proper timing, correct body placement when punching, and the wind and skill required, by many hard workouts with all types of sparring partners, building your confidence and punching authority, punch by punch!

There are many **boxing styles**, most styles are a combination of one or more of the basic styles, which are, the <u>puncher</u>, a sort of Joe Louis type, the <u>boxer</u>, a sort of Muhammad Ali type, the <u>slugger</u>, a Rocky Marciano or Joe Frazier type, or the <u>brawler</u>, a Tex Cobb or Chuck Wepner type, these are only examples. There are many more, along with the combinations and variations of styles. Whichever style you more or less resemble, try to be an intellectual fighter. Great fighters have been copied and imitated but never duplicated.

In boxing you are your own man, you may have a superior corner, the one with more knowledge and experience, and this may or may not win the fight for you. Although this is certainly a big advantage, when the bell rings its mano-a-mano, (hand to hand) and there will be three minutes before you will receive any instructions from your corner (Note: Fig. #309).

This reminds me of a time when I was much younger and a friend of mine needed help in preparing for a semi-final bout in a golden glove match. I was busy with other things but put them aside to help a good friend. I worked with him for 8 days getting him ready for his next bout. Two minutes before his fight he spotted a trainer he once knew and asked me if <u>he</u> could take my place in the corner as his adviser or the chief second. I replied "if you want" so my friend listened to this other guys advise and fight plan while I only assisted in the corner, but this other trainer didn't really know my friends style or abilities therefore his advice wasn't beneficial. This other trainer looked at me during the last round for advice to now instruct my friend, but it was too late.

Never change camps or trainers or boats in mid-stream; my friend was knocked out that night in the last round much to the credit of shifting advisors or trainers.

Boxing is <u>not</u> a game where you can <u>pass</u> <u>the</u> <u>ball</u>, to relieve some of the pressure, or slip the baton to your teammate in the middle of a bout! Each and every round of boxing is an <u>all-out</u> three minute <u>war</u>! Learn how to box from a knowledgeable instructor, one who knows <u>you</u> and <u>your</u> <u>style</u> and adhere to their advice. Also get into the proper condition <u>before</u> entering the ring for any actual bouts and if you train with a certain team, trainer or adviser have them in your corner and advising <u>you</u> at fight time!

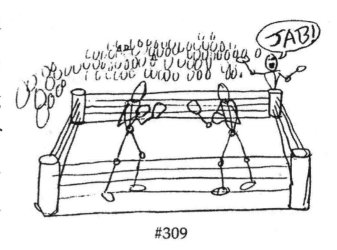

#309

Remember, all styles of fighting are modified to suit that individual boxer and should also be modified occasionally when fighting against certain opponents, it's important to be versatile; being able to adapt to situations as they arise and styles as they change. Not to confuse you, but great fighters will change their fighting styles in order to obtain the advantage. Example: It's important to oppose the opposite tactics to those favored by your opponent, box a puncher, counter a boxer, box a slugger etc. Unless you are certain you can out box the boxer or out punch the puncher or out slug the slugger. If you make the wrong decision, you will soon know. For instance, the first round may prove that you may have started with the right tactics, but your opponent had the right solution, so adapt, adapt, adapt!

Using <u>only</u> your <u>left</u> or <u>only</u> your <u>right</u>, makes you only a <u>one</u> handed fighter, that's like eating rice without the beans, throw in the beans, always be a <u>two</u> fisted fighter, keeping your opponent in complete puzzlement, having him only wonder what your next punch or move is. A fighter who relies on his defense, is called a <u>counter</u> <u>puncher</u>, this is a fighter who waits for <u>you</u> to throw punches <u>first</u>, so he can masterfully counter your punches, to his advantage. In this instance it may be best to draw <u>his</u> lead, attempting to mix up his strategy or tactics in your favor through feints. Keeping the pressure on this type fighter by throwing your punches with "<u>rhyme and reason</u>" without much let up, then move away.

Boxing is like a chess game, to know when, where, and how, for how long, how hard or how fast will all take time, patience, gym work, and much practice! (Note: Fig. #310).

#310

When fighting against a slugger type fighter and you are a boxer, and he cuts off the ring or corners you – and he is past your punching range: Remember, the pole in my garage, don't slug with him; tie him up (clinch) until the referee breaks you. Fight him at a distance, if he rushes in, sidestep and counter, movement is the key, have him fight your fight, be persistent!

If you're a fighter with a bobbing and weaving style, one that adds rapid head movement to it, head movement that resembles a triangle or a square or whatever (Note: Fig. #311) mix it up constantly. If you don't, your opponent will use your head action, to his advantage, timing your constant repetitious head movement with his punches.

#311

While an opponent who relies on strong and speedy attacks or flights in flurries, you should attack without much let up, right after one of his flurries, but of course, your defense must be in order!

A boxer with a long reach, or a fighter who constantly attacks with a step forward, generally requires some room. Therefore if you are always stepping back while he is attacking, you are giving your opponent the room he requires to maneuver, so if you step forward with a snappy movement or sideways, a lateral movement, then counter his lead, you will off balance his attack in your favor.

When fighting an orthodox fighter, that's forced to fight southpaw momentarily, because of your pressure or it may be of his choice, either way, this could be the best time to execute your attack. Most orthodox fighters do <u>not</u> fight or defend nearly as well when switching to southpaw. Unless of course he's a converted southpaw, it's always <u>wise</u> to know or learn all you can about an opponent <u>before</u> fighting him!

When fighting a southpaw it may help to let him lead with his right jab, slip or sidestep the punch to your left side and counter with your left hook to his body or head. Right hand leads are also effective against the southpaw while circling to your left, followed by your left hook. As I stated earlier, if there is any awkwardness for you, it should be just as awkward for him, except for the fact that the <u>southpaw</u> <u>fighter</u> is much more accustomed to the sort of opposition he encounters. Southpaw fighters, fight mostly <u>orthodox</u> <u>fighters</u>.

What is required of the orthodox fighter is a great deal of practice in sparring southpaw fighters, getting acquainted with the difference and becoming accustomed to this mirror image. If you lack the experience needed to fight and win against a southpaw and you have a choice avoid them, until you're properly prepared to fight one.

You will be at a big disadvantage in a bout, if you're not properly schooled and have little to no experience sparring southpaws, southpaw's usually only spar orthodox fighters, simply because there are mostly orthodox fighters in the world.

This alone gives the southpaw a big advantage, example; if both fighters' abilities are equal and the orthodox fighter has little, not enough, or no experience sparring with southpaws, the southpaw would win. This reminds me of the fight between Evander Holyfield and Michael Moorer on April 22, 1994 in Las Vegas, Nevada. Evander Holyfield just didn't have enough experience to fight the southpaw Michael Moorer. Moorer became the WBA and IBF heavyweight champion that night; mainly because he was a southpaw fighter.

Fighting against an opponent who seems awkward or sloppy, who may use wide and unexpected punches, his rhythm is most likely irregular, and it's hard to judge his attack, his lack of style may be the only style you know nothing about!

If you want to beat this opponent without looking equally sloppy, don't use advanced moves, you will never know what he may do, or not do next. Therefore, use simple, quick, fundamental attacks. To lose a match against such an opponent, shows you may lack the ability to adapt your style to the requirements of the moment, learn to adapt. This will come in time through constant training and practicing using the many movements learned in this book. Remember, they all derive from the basics and fundamentals.

The fighter whose movements seem awkward is the one who never seems to find his punches reaching his target. The fighter who is always telegraphing his punches, or overshooting his target, this fighter may be suffering from a lack of coordination.

This fighter must go back to the basics, the fundamentals, and start over! The well-coordinated fighter's moves are all smooth and graceful. He seems to glide over the canvas with little or no effort. This fighters timing is usually on the mark, because his own body movements are controlled, and each made with a purpose in mind. His punches are not just thrown with the hope of landing, they're thrown with "rhyme and reason" along with confidence and good judgment!

I remember this small part in a western movie called "Butch Cassidy and the Sundance Kid", I will use as an example to amplify my meaning. A man throws a small tobacco snuffbox about 25 feet onto the ground in front of him. He then asked Sundance, Robert Redford to shoot and hit the snuffbox, by simply standing still and aiming at it. Sundance misses badly, Sundance then asks, "Can I move?" the man replies "move?", "what the hell you mean move?" Sundance re-holsters his gun, and this time draws it from his holster rapidly, simultaneously bending at the waist, firing two shots, hitting his target both times. Sundance then said, "I'm better when I move." Quick, accurate, and well-coordinated moves are what boxing is all about! Most times you're punching a moving target or you're punching while you yourself are moving; learn to punch in motion!

 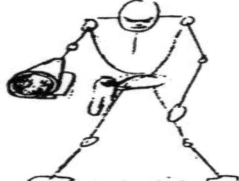

Incidentally, if you have to push your hair out of your eyes, wipe sweat from your face, or look at the referee momentarily do it quickly and out of the reach of your opponent!

If you have to cover up because of a rally of punches thrown by your opponent, do so and move, know what's happening. Turn defense into offense by sidestepping, ducking, slipping or parrying, always countering and attacking with confidence. Try to control the pace of the fight, dictating your authority, see yourself as a master craftsman in the boxing ring!

All fighters are unique and should be trained differently to some degree, but all, should be taught the fundamentals in all the basic styles, in offense and defense. To defend against them and to be victorious over them!

One who participates if even only on a training level, in the sport of boxing whether for fun or profit may be arguably labeled or referred to as; a boxer, a fighter, a pugilist or pug, a contender, a prize fighter, a fisticuffer, a scrapper, a warrior, a champ, a palooka, a chump, a tomato can or a bum.

But, the style of a particular fighter leaves little room for argument; these styles are as follows, along with some other rather discriminative phrases and my definition for each.

1) **Puncher**- stand up fighter, plants his feet firmly on the canvas and proceeds to throw hard punches in good combination.

2) **Boxer**- stand up fighter, has good movement, slips punches well, uses side to side movement and fading back to avoid opponent's punches, can punch while moving and is elusive.

3) **Slugger**- crouching down type fighter, always moving towards his opponent, has good bobbing and weaving ability, throws punches from a crouched position, using his legs for extra leverage, usually a hard banger, with a poor jab but power house hooks. Likes to muscle himself in close to his opponent and bang away!

4) **Brawler**- crouch down fighter, somewhat like a slugger, but more erratic, throws swings at times in place of crisp punches, never stops coming at his opponent, has no jab.

5) **Boxer/Dancer**- Stand up fighter, like the boxer but his foot movements are a thing of beauty, does not plant feet as often as the boxer, good timing, and usually frustrates opponents by his constant movement. Hits and moves, hits and moves, is elusive.

6) **Street fighter**- Unpredictable, inconsistent, fights dirty and will do anything to win, unskilled, lacking the ingredients for the boxing ring and has no sportsmanship.

7) **Counter puncher**- Schooled in countering each boxing punch thrown by any type fighter. Excellent defensive strategist, will wait for opponents lead using that lead to launch his own attack. Boring fight if his opponent is also a counter puncher.

8) **A Survivor**- A fighter that's in there to simply go through the motions can take a good punch, make his opponent look good, and do just enough to lose a fight.

9) **A Journeyman**- Is somewhat like the survivor, but gives a consistently fair account of himself and occasionally wins a fight, usually in there to build up his opponent's record.

10) **A Runner**- A fighter who is always on his "bicycle" will keep moving or dancing away from his opponent throughout the fight, avoiding any possible confrontation, making it a dull fight or no fight at all.

11) **A Body puncher**- A fighter who attacks the body, but does it constantly and in an effective manner.

12) **A Head hunter**- A fighter who attacks the head and the head only, neglecting his opponent's body.

13) **A Sparring partner**- This fighter is stuck in a sparring partner syndrome, he is content to only spar and he brings this "way" with him to his boxing matches, this fighter lacks "RHYME & REASON."

14) **A Contender**- This is a world class, quality fighter one that is ready to fight for the title, possibly in the top ten. A fighter that would be a worthy competitor for the world championship.

15) **A Loser**- This is a fighter, who will for whatever reason go on fighting and fighting, but rarely wins and usually has more losses than wins, every fighter wants to fight him, to build up their own record. He will take fights on little notice, or no notice at all, will fight in or out of shape, fighting for the pay day. Has a limited supply of boxing skills, usually lacking in the basics and fundamentals, stepping stone for poor to good fighters.

16) Then, there's the <u>has been's</u>, the <u>could be's</u>, the <u>should be's</u> and the <u>want to be's</u>. You can conclude your own analysis of these…

Many a time you will see a fighter being a composite of more than one of the above categories or styles, sometimes changing in the middle of a fight from one to the other, in order to adapt to his opponent's strengths or weaknesses, this is the sign of a mature fighter, a well-schooled fighter, one that has boxing knowledge and experience, using whatever will work against his opponent at that time to win that bout!

All fighters fall into one of these categories or styles, some may fall into two, three or more of these at the same time! What is most important is that you learn to acknowledge which category you fall into, recognize one from the other and what it would take to win against each of them.

The **ring** <u>size</u>, many a time has an effect on the outcome of a fight. A ring 18 feet squared or less will greatly favor the slugger, brawler, street fighter and body puncher because they all would rather fight you in a broom closet! The smaller the better, allowing them to use their relentless style to cut off the ring, so they may catch you and do their intended damage with less effort, because even a turtle can catch a rabbit if the box is small enough (Note: Fig. #312).

Likewise, the boxing rings 18 feet squared or more favor the runner, the boxer, the counter puncher, boxer/dancer, and the puncher, because these fighters require more room to fight at their best, for lateral movement, in and out movement and punching with movement, the more room the better, frustrating their opponent, especially if he's doing the chasing (Note: Fig. #313).

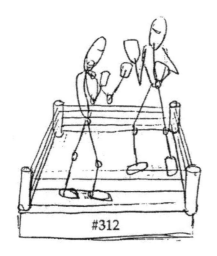

#312

#313

The <u>rings</u> <u>flooring</u> can also affect the outcome of a fight. A firm canvas floor will favor the runner, the boxer/dancer, counter puncher, puncher and crafty boxer. This type of flooring will allow them to move with grace and ease, in and out, left and right and around and around. A surface that's unyielding will benefit and compliment fast movement. When the boxer moving from one direction to another can simply move without having to sink into the flooring first, his movement is faster.

Likewise, soft canvas flooring will slow down the fight by absorbing all foot movement transferring the floor into a doughy mushy surface, hurting the fast fighter and giving the slugger, brawler, body puncher or slower fighter an advantage. Soft flooring would be somewhat like boxing in mud! (Note: Fig #314, #315)

#314

#315

The ring ropes can also affect a fight. Three ropes give less support than four ropes; loose ropes give no bounce back and no support. Tight ropes will favor the runner, the boxer/dancer, counter puncher and crafty boxer by enabling them to utilize the ropes to their advantage. They do this by bouncing off them in such a way as to offset their opponent's pace, or by turning their opponent around using the ropes as in a spring boarding effect, escaping their opponent's attack, or utilizing the ropes to catapult their own attack (Note: Fig. #316).

Likewise, the ropes when loose or not firm will benefit the slugger, brawler, street fighter, body puncher, and less polished or slower fighter because ropes that are loose, giving no support will cause the fighter that's thrust upon them, to go nowhere but down! (Note: Fig. #317).

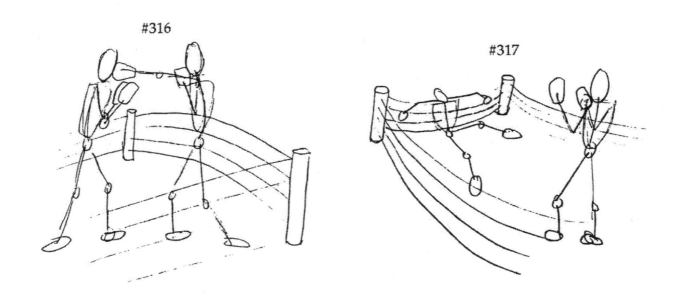

#316   #317

One instance, when firm ropes benefited a fighter greatly is when Muhammad Ali fought George Foreman in Kinshasa, Zaire on October 30, 1974. Ali used the ropes to hold himself up and support himself while Foreman tired himself out punching Ali's body and arms. All the while, Ali covered up and kept his back against the firm ropes, he labeled this his "rope-a-dope" trick. The outcome of that fight was, Muhammad Ali regaining the Heavyweight Championship, very much to the credit of firm ropes. If you don't believe me, "let's go to the video tape!" or today it would be the DVD, or You Tube!

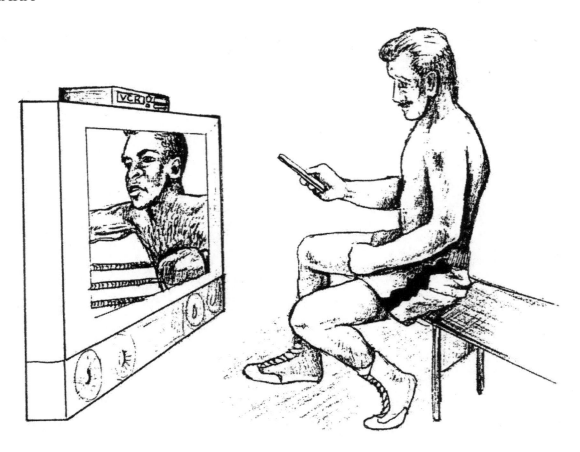

In an actual bout you should always fight as if your very life depends on it, you shouldn't be one to quit.

If you're getting mugged, or beaten badly in the ring, change your style, listen to your corner, and fight harder. If the fight is going to be stopped, let the <u>referee</u> stop it, and he will, as soon as he can see you're being beaten badly and you're <u>not</u> fighting back. But, that's his decision, <u>not</u> yours. <u>Your</u> <u>mind</u> should be focused on beating the man in front of you, not on where you should fall down, or when you should quit. Try throwing your punches from different angles using a different approach toward your offense and defense, finding what will work against <u>that</u> opponent may only be one punch away, Don't quit! Overcome!

I have seen many professional fighters lose heart and quit in the middle of a fight, for no apparent reason. As if they had placed a large bet down <u>against</u> themselves, or if their check had already cleared, so <u>they're</u> tired and want to go home now. Don't <u>you</u> give up, give it your <u>all</u>, always!

This reminds me of the third Muhammad Ali vs. Joe Frazier fight on September 30, 1975. By the end of the 10th round, Ali gave serious thoughts of quitting. "I felt like I was dying," said Ali. But, summoning up more courage than he knew he had, Ali continued to fight on. Ali successfully defended his heavyweight championship title that night, largely because he battled on <u>past</u> the point of giving up and would <u>not</u> quit!

Another fighter that showed the **will to press on** was George Foreman. Two months away from his 46th birthday or older, a 3 to 1 underdog but irrespective to what many felt; on November 5, 1994 recaptured the heavyweight championship for the second time at 2:03 of the 10th round at the MGM Grand in Las Vegas, beating Michael Moore, who was 26 years old; this win came twenty years and six days after George Forman lost it to Muhammad Ali, in Zaire.

George Foreman on that night became the oldest man ever to win the W.B.A & I.B.F heavyweight championship, largely because of his determination and using the will to press on!

Yes, winning any bout could only be one punch away! Ask big George Foreman, he'll tell you…PRESS ON!!

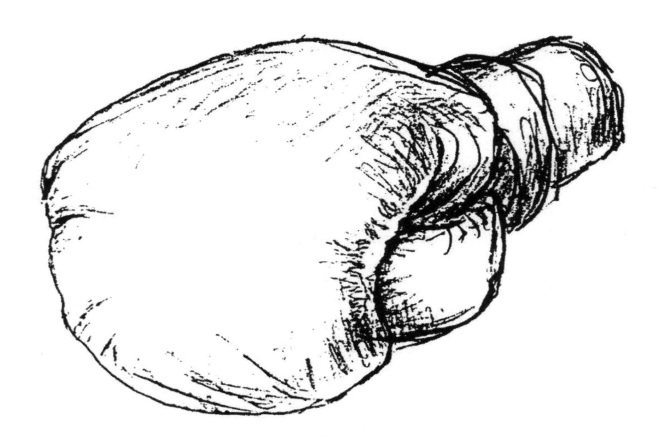

Chapter 8

* ALL ABOUT TRAINERS *

Most trainers are only one dimensional which produces only mechanical fighters. Who are fighters that cannot change or adapt to certain conditions or situations as they occur. This trainer may have had one successful boxer at that particular style, so he believes he should train all of his fighters that way. This type of trainer may have fought that way when he was boxing, once upon a time, or was taught only his style and cannot adapt his training techniques for different fighting styles.

The trainers who train and teach all fighters the same style, not taking into account what style his fighter feels best at or is most suited for, like the fighter's body type or build, his reach or coordination, or lack of it, can do more damage than good to these fighters. A boxing trainer should <u>not</u> just "keep time" while his student is training, the trainer should instruct, just as a martial arts master would instruct his pupil in the fine arts, so it should be in the fine art of boxing. If a trainer doesn't seem to know, show or teach the fighter, this fighter must leave that trainer. He can ruin this fighter, especially if this fighter has any potential or future ambitions in boxing at all. There may of course be rare exceptions, the fighter may fit the mold of this trainer, and be outstanding at his particular style of fighting, because he hasn't been schooled properly on how to adapt to any others.

What I truly recommend for any fighter entering the ring, especially professionals is to be schooled in all styles and the counters for each style, along with the ability to change that style immediately if needed to win the bout (Note: Fig. #318).

#318

Here's an example: Let's say you're a slugger and so is your opponent, but he is beating you in your own style, fighting your fight, which is also his fighting style, and his fight but he is better than you. Continuing with your present style or way of fighting you will definitely lose. To win you must now adapt, change styles, possibly to a boxer or puncher. This will throw your opponent off, hopefully changing the flow and outcome of the fight. But instead, round after round you march back to your corner and your trainer gives you the same poor instructions, or none at all, and each round your opponent is dishing you out a bad beating. The trainer you have believes your opponent is simply a much better fighter than you are this may or may not be the case.

If your trainer only knew how to alter your technique, your style, and if you were trained to do so <u>before</u> the bout, you now will be able to adapt. Either leave your trainer if you feel he cannot train you properly in <u>all</u> styles, <u>offensively</u> and <u>defensively</u>, or give him a copy of my book, and have him study it!

There are trainers who will literally worm their way into some fighters life, just to get that fighter hurt or worse due to their greed, ignorance or both! Beware of trainers who want you to spar when you're <u>not</u> at all ready, they will <u>use</u> <u>you</u> to build up their fighter's confidence, having their more experienced or in shape fighters beat up on you!

Beware of trainers who suggest they know all the moves, or say when seeing a certain block or combination, "that's one of my moves." Boxing and its moves have been around for centuries!

A large percentage of fighter's are lost in the fighter's own corner due to incompetent trainers and corner men. When your fighter returns to his corner have his stool ready for him to sit down. Keep the fighter's arms at his sides, not on the ropes. Take out his mouth piece and have him rinse his mouth, and then drink some water. Now, would be the time to instruct your fighter on what he may be doing wrong, and most important what he has to do right now; to win the fight! Keep instructions simple, direct and to the point. Don't yell, curse or shout at your fighter, look him straight in the eye and make certain he comprehends what you're saying.

No one else in this corner should be talking to the fighter but the trainer. Too many voices instructing him will confuse the fighter. The trainer must take control of the corner, and his fighter, during that one minute interval, all the while himself or preferably a corner assistant is tending to any ailments or cuts the fighter may have suffered during the course of the fight.

A good trainer will bring you along slowly, work you out regularly, only allow you to spar when he believes your truly ready and you yourself know you're ready. Choosing a sparring partner that will only help you in your quest for boxing knowledge. An experienced fighter, one that could hold back and help you rather than hurt you.

A good trainer will let you train with this fighter first on only blocking your jab, then your only blocking his, throwing all punches in slow motion alternating offense and defense. Then working other punches and their counters one at a time, before actually letting you spar and do your own thing, at your own pace (refer to Chapter 6).

A good trainer will be able to train you in your best suited style, teaching you to recognize every other style and train you properly enabling you to defend successfully and win against all of them.

A good trainer will train you seriously throughout the three minute work bell and not rattle on about irrelevant subjects while you're training. He should <u>not</u> talk about anything not relating to your training while you're working out. Keeping his complete focus towards <u>your</u> boxing improvements!

A good trainer, when preparing for any actual boxing matches, will select his fighter's opponent's with extreme caution, choosing only opponent's his fighter can more than likely beat, building up his fighter's confidence. Slowly moving towards opponent's with more talent, but only when his fighter is ready. A good trainer should arrive at the event early, making certain the ropes and flooring will benefit his fighter. If at all possible, beforehand insisting on the size of the ring to benefit his fighter. Having all the proper equipment in order, his and yours.

His being, a water bottle filled with cold water, a bucket, hand gauze, tape, first aid kit, solution to stop bleeding, bandage scissors, ice bag filled with ice, sponge, cotton swabs, petroleum jelly, latex gloves, towels and a cold compress, or (stainless steel device that helps to reduce swelling)

The fighter's equipment includes a mouthpiece, foul protector, boxing trunks, robe, boxing shoes, a pair of underwear, pair of socks, gym bag with a change of clothes and an autograph pen! I'm only joking about the pen. If the bout is an amateur bout, headgear may be required.

The ring, ring stool, ring stairs, the timer, the bell, ring cards, card girl, boxing gloves, referee, officials and such should be provided by the fighting organization sponsoring the event. (Note: Fig. #319)

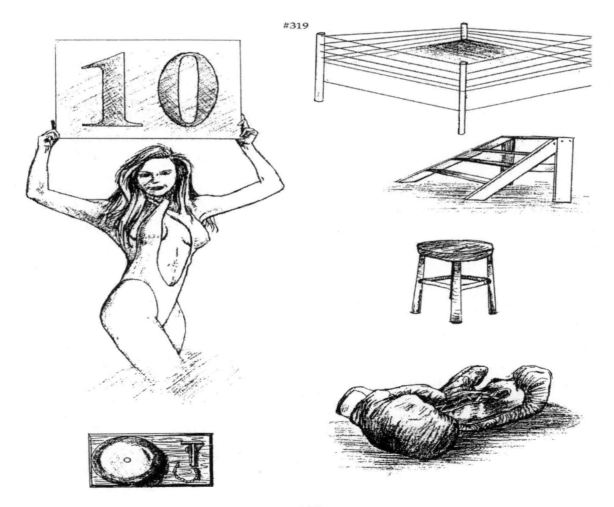

#319

Chapter 9

* WEIGHT TRAINING *

Boxers will develop a strong punch through the constant and proper training, provided by punching a heavy bag. The punching muscles, shoulders, triceps as well as the upper back and lats can be developed more quickly by weight training. I recommend weight training each body part only once a week, thereby, giving your muscles adequate <u>time to recover and grow</u>, on a three or four day routine. One custom made for you or similar to the example below:

Day 1 – Triceps and shoulders
Day 2 – Back (Latissimus Dorsi) lats and neck
Day 3 – OFF
Day 4 – Chest and biceps
Day 5 – OFF
Day 6 – Legs and arms
Day 7 – OFF

There are many combinations and variations of weight training programs. The key is not to overstrain "less is best" when it comes to weight training for boxing. What usually happens is we will train, over train and injure! This holds true for all weight training, boxing and aerobic workouts as well! Skill and endurance training are the most important when it comes to boxing.

All training workouts should fall between 30 to 50 minutes each, more than this puts undo strain on the body and prevents muscle development. This is very important; muscles grow when you rest, not when you train. Rest is anabolic (will construct) and training is catabolic (will breakdown). If you train or workout too much or too frequently, you're always tearing down tissue and never allowing enough time for repair or growth! Train with <u>strict</u> <u>form</u> <u>and</u> <u>maximum</u> <u>intensity</u>, working out the larger muscles is most important, but afterwards so is <u>adequate</u> <u>rest</u>. Full range of motion is also important to ensure that the entire length of the muscle is developed.

The four basic movements are squats, dead lift, bench press and military press. You can perform only these exercises if you want, adding others to them gradually. If weight machines are available you may use them, but free weights will bring faster results. Build a foundation of muscle with these compound movements first, before going on to the full program. When you're familiar with weight training, add or subtract to the program or make up your own! Isolation movements such as wrist curls, toe raises, etc. etc. could be added on later if needed.

Always exhale while you're doing the pushing or pulling, the actual lift, <u>inhaling</u> on the down stroke of the movement or when returning the weight to the <u>original</u> position.

When returning the weight to its original starting position, <u>slow</u> this part of the movement down, for instance, when doing a bench press, (working **chest**) bring the weight down to your chest taking 3 to 4 seconds and back up taking 1 to 2 seconds; concentrating on the <u>negative</u> part of the movement will bring you much <u>faster</u> <u>results</u> (Note: Fig. #320 - #323).

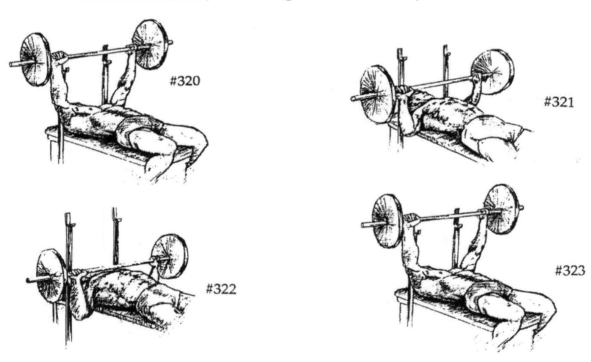

<u>Each movement is called a repetition or rep and each group of reps are called a set</u>. Experiment with the weights, in most cases find a weight you can do 7 reps with, but just barely, work with this weight until you do 11 reps with it. Then add more weight to your

dumbbells or barbell, bringing the reps of that exercise back down to 7 reps. Continue with this weight until you can perform 11 reps again, and so on.

Using progressively heavier weights builds bigger muscles, so increase weight whenever possible. Use this formula unless otherwise instructed. Shown are some of the many exercises that will benefit the punching muscles. Never forget to <u>warm up first</u> at least 5-10 minutes as stated earlier. Then duplicate the moves you will do during your workout, using much lighter weights, this will assure you that your muscles are totally warmed up. Starting with dumbbells, dumbbells are excellent for boxers because they're independent and more closely resemble punching movements.

The alternating dumbbell press works the **<u>shoulders</u>** and **<u>triceps</u>**. I like to do them seated on a bench with my back against it for support, but they can also be done standing as well, 7-11 reps, 1-2 sets (Note: Fig. #324 - #325). I've worked up to using 100 lbs. dumbbells in each hand for 7 reps, while weighing 162lbs. Still throwing 7 jabs per second, this is to inform all critics that believe weight training will slow you down; if you work out properly, it might just speed your punches up a bit!

#324

#325

The military press or (front barbell press) also targets the **shoulders** and **triceps**, make certain you lift the weight properly, to do so, first bend your knees, keeping your head upright, looking straight forward (Note: Fig. #326). Bring the weight up to your shoulders (Note: Fig. #327), now, <u>without</u> bending your knees, press the weight overhead (Note: Fig. #328). Bring the weight back to your shoulders and stop, lift overhead again (Note: Fig. #329), each time the weight is moved from your shoulders to overhead is considered one rep, 7-11 reps, 1-2 sets.

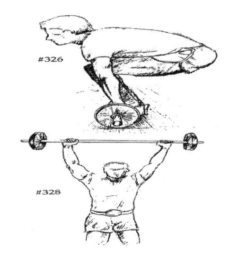

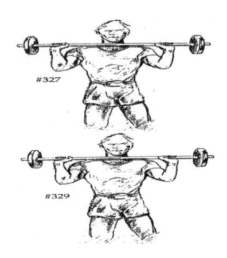

Shoulders will receive a great workout doing side raises (lateral raises) (Note: Fig. #330, #331), this works the outside muscles of each shoulder (side and rear deltoids), with this exercise use dumbbells and do 10-15 reps, 1-2 sets.

Alternating front raises (Note: Fig. #332 - #333) also using dumbbells. This works the front shoulder muscles (front deltoids), do 10-15 reps, 1-2 sets.

Tricep extensions when performed using proper form is a good exercise isolating the triceps muscle, they can be done either standing or seated, exercise one arm at a time using a dumbbell.

Keep your shoulder as vertical as possible bringing the weight down as shown, and back up 10-15 reps, 1-2 sets (Note: Fig. #334 - #335).

For **back** and **neck** workouts, start with pull-ups (two sets of twenty) or your best effort. (Note: Fig. #336, #337). Using a lat machine (Note: Fig. #338, #339), do behind the neck pull downs seated, keeping arms just slightly wider than your shoulders width is best 7-11 reps, 1-2 sets. Also a great exercise for the back muscles are floor seated rows (Note: Fig. #340,#341), 7-11 reps, 1-2 sets.

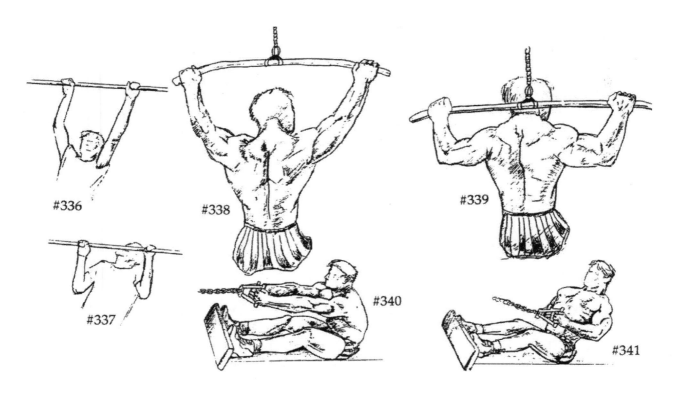

When doing <u>deadlifts</u> (**lower back**) gluteus, quadriceps, hamstrings, keep your knees slightly bent, barbell as close to your body as possible, back straight and head upright, using a weight lifting belt to be safe, using a reverse grip (one palm up, one palm down) or you can use a regular grip. When lowering the weight during your reps, don't touch the floor with the barbell until you're ready to put the weight down completing that set (Note: Fig. #342 - #346), 7-11 reps, 1-2 sets.

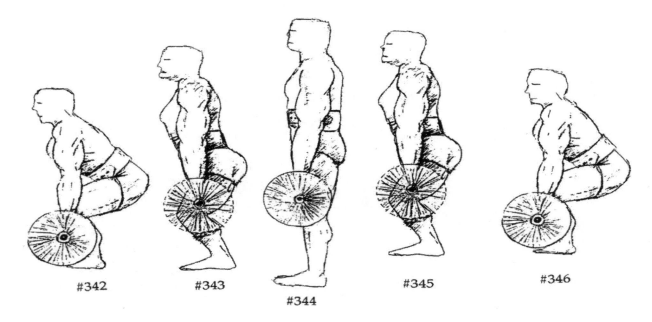

#342   #343   #344   #345   #346

If a gym is not available or the equipment to do lat pulls and seated rows, you can do <u>dumbbell rows</u> (for Back) in their place. Keeping one hand on bench for support, back straight, head facing down, bring the dumbbell straight up and down (repeat for opposite arm) (Note: Fig. #347, #348), 7-11 reps, 1-2 sets.

The <u>dumbbell shrug</u> is one of the best exercises for developing your trapezius and <u>neck</u> muscles, keep your arms and back straight, chest out, head facing forward, raise your shoulders as <u>high</u> as possible then lower them as <u>low</u> as possible.

(Note: Fig. #349 - #351), 10-15 reps, 2-3 sets.

A <u>head strap</u>, one that allows you to add weights to it will also build up your <u>neck</u> muscles. At first, do only 1 set, but higher reps 15-25, seated is best, go slow with this one (Note: Fig. #352 - #354). There are other ways to build up your neck muscles for instance Sonny Liston stood on his head about a half hour a day, while

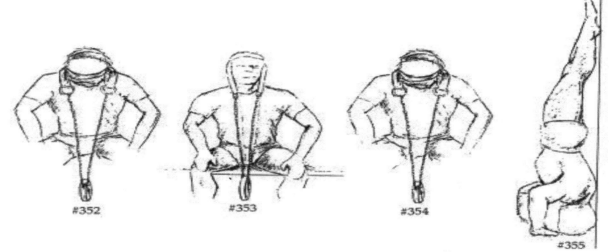

training for a fight (Note: Fig. #355)

This is called an incline bench press and it will build your <u>upper</u> <u>chest</u> muscles (upper pectorals) (Note: Fig. #356, #357), 7-11 reps, 2-3 sets.

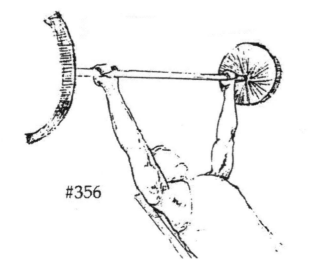

This is called a decline bench press and it will build up the lower part of your chest (lower pectorals) (Note: Fig. #358 - #359), 7-11 reps, 2-3 sets. When doing all or any bench pressing exercises it's wise to have someone there to "spot you," helping if need be with that very last rep. If this isn't possible be very careful, especially when doing that last rep, the one you think you might be able to do. Yes, it's the most important rep, working the muscle fibers that are the hardest to reach, but it's not as important as your life!

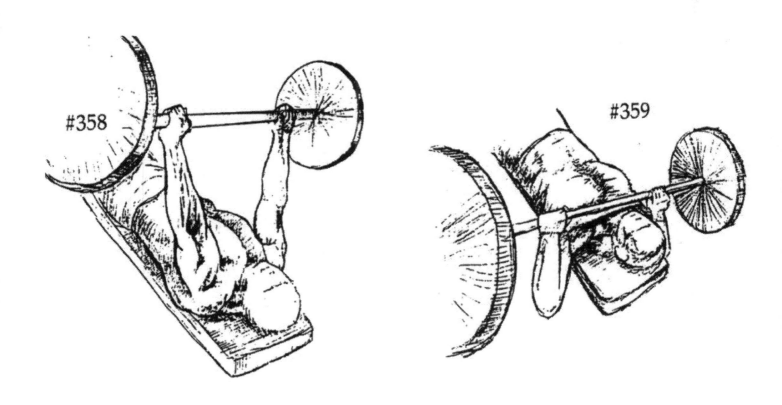

#358

#359

The flat bench press (Note: Fig. #360, #361), 7-11 reps, 2-3 sets. Dumbbells, may be substituted lying on the flat bench, both exercises will work your <u>chest</u> muscles (pectorals), (Note: Fig. #362, #363).

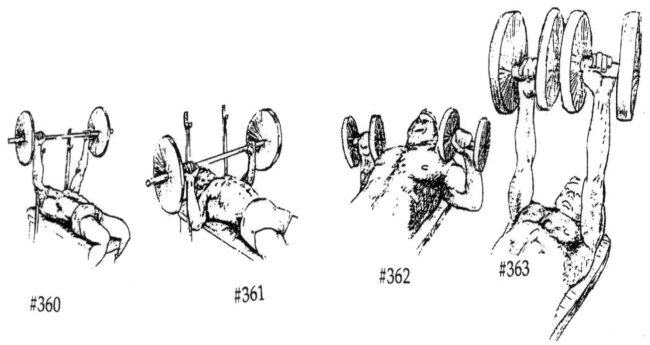

#360 #361 #362 #363

When building up your chest, you will add strength that can be used in pushing off your opponent at close range. Inches will also be added and this may help pad the chest area, cushioning punches aimed at the very vulnerable spot of chest, your <u>solar plexus</u> (Note: Fig. #364).

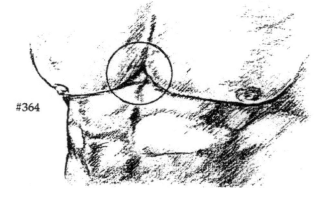

#364

The bicep and back can be worked by doing **chin-ups** (Note: Fig. #365 - #366), (two sets of twenty) or your best effort. I reached **my personal best in 2020, 44 reps, yes without stopping! My new goal is 50!** *Picture on page 136*

Seated <u>dumbbell curls</u>, keeping back against bench will help to take the swing out of this exercise, eliminating a cheating effect, this exercise also works the biceps (Note: Fig. #367 - #369), 7-11 reps 2-3 sets.

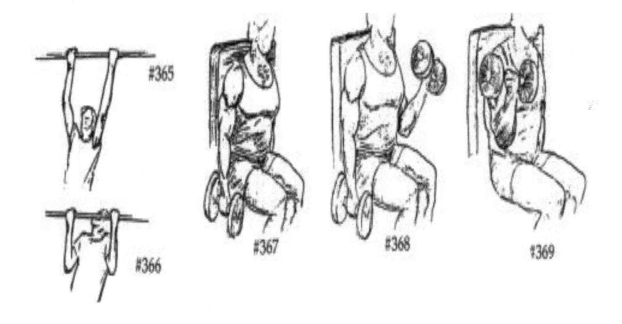

Barbell curls, while standing wearing your weight lifting belt to be safe, as with all curls bend your elbows, but keep your upper arms motionless against your sides. This exercise also works your biceps (Note: Fig. #370 - #371).

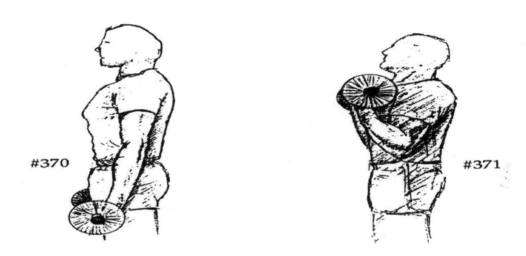

When working your legs, I recommend using a squat machine (leg press) (Note: Fig. #372, #373), 7-11 reps, 2-3 sets. Keeping your back against the cushion assures you of not injuring your back. When using a barbell to perform squats, only go down to a <u>parallel position</u>, to avoid possible knee injury, and to make certain of this you can use a bench or chair underneath you. Keep your back as straight as possible while moving up and down. Keep all your body weight over the center of your feet, placing a board or 2x4 under your heels may help. The objective is to keep your shins as vertical as possible, and wear your weight lifting belt for safety (Note: Fig. #374, #375)

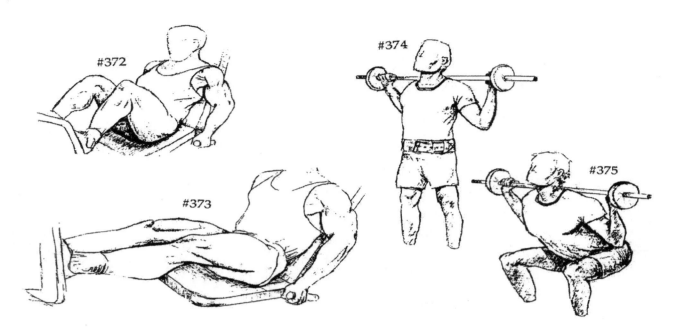

Another good exercise for **legs** that does not require a gym, are lunges. Using dumbbells, take a small step forward, keeping a dumbbell in each hand, squat half-way down and alternate your legs. Don't lean forward when you step, instead keep your upper body in line with your hips. Stepping forward so that your knee of your lead leg is directly over the heel of that lead foot (Note: Fig. #376 - #379), 10-15 reps, 2-3 sets.

Leg extensions, using a leg extension machine (this exercise works the quadriceps), both legs at one time or one leg at a time (Note: Fig. #380 - #382), 7-11 reps, 1-2 sets. Hamstrings can be worked usually using the same leg extension machine at home, or if at the gym, their hamstring machine (leg curl) (Note: Fig. #383, #384), 7-11 reps, 2-3 sets

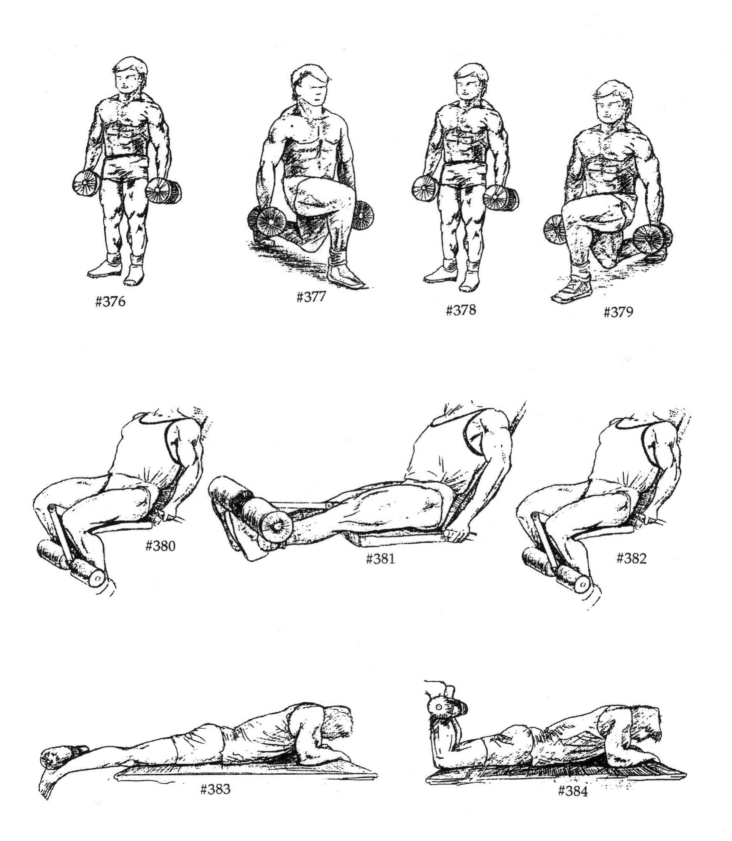

#376

#377

#378

#379

#380

#381

#382

#383

#384

Remember; try to find an amount that will enable you to do 7-11 reps, 2-3 sets on most of the exercises unless otherwise mentioned. Your intensity level must be very high in order to achieve desirable results. If the weight you're using can be lowered in a slow controlled manner as it should, it's too heavy, and if you can do 7 reps too easily, the weights are too light. If you're not completely putting all your best efforts into your workouts, you're only fooling yourself and wasting your time. Slow progression is the key to long term results! Don't rush with weight training; just try to keep making progress. When you reach a plateau make changes in your routine, and if at this point your progress still seems stuck like a "bill in Congress," try taking off 7 to 10 days and relax, before commencing with your workouts.

For boxers most leg workouts consist of running and rope jumping. This is all boxers in the past ever required, in fact if you train your legs too much with weights; you will find an increase in body weight. This may be good or bad, for instance in the lighter weight class, you may find it a problem keeping your weight down. In boxing, your legs are the single most important part of your body, they are your foundation! Keep them in shape!

If you are looking to gain weight you should workout with weights and you should exercise the larger muscles first. The legs, chest and back, while working these muscles you will find all other muscles growing in proportion to your body.

As far as weight lifting is concerned and you're a boxer, for instance in the lighter weight divisions, and you're trying to gain muscle weight to move up into a higher weight class, weight lifting is the answer. It will be a tremendous help.

You should also ingest your regular caloric amount one day and on the next day try ingesting 500 – 750 calories more. Fluctuating this, but always keeping your fat intake low and increase your protein intake to 1.5 to 1.75 grams per pound of your current body weight. If you are just trying to maintain your weight but want additional power, try doing less working out with weights but don't leave them on the floor entirely. Yes, I am a firm believer that weight training is a great asset for all boxers!

What I show in this book are some basic exercises. There are many more for each body part, use what applies most to your body type, your needs, or what will help you in your weak areas. Remember, the simple fact, boxing is neither a weight lifting tournament, nor a tug of war and the man with the biggest muscles or best looking body doesn't always win. Speed combined with the properly executed basic fundamentals will 99 out of 100 times conquer any opponent using only brute strength!

Remember the equation, <u>Power</u> = <u>Speed</u> x <u>Force</u>.

For the people worrying about getting too big, too bulky or too slow, because of some muscle growth from weight training, need not worry, that's like suggesting after reading this book,
you'll be too dangerous to walk the streets! That's just not reality! As long as you practice speed movements, shadow boxing and working on technique there should be no loss of speed by the gaining of muscle.

Incidentally, never use weights in your gloves or hands while punching, this could lead to injury. This exercise program will help strengthen your body. Don't get obsessed with weight training, use it as an aid. Some fighters have great builds, dislike weight training and may only need boxing specific work. For these fighters, I recommend doing 30 minutes of **calisthenics** 4 days a week in addition to their boxing workout (Refer to page 145).

Never forget to work out your **abdominal** or stomach area daily. There are many ways to build up your stomach area but remember, while building up that area we don't want to hurt or injure any other areas, such as the lower back. Many athletes in the process of building up one area, injure another. For the stomach, I recommend the crunch (Note: Fig. #385, #386) keeping your lower back on the floor, just raising your upper back, keeping stomach muscles tight while moving in each direction. This exercise will benefit the abdominal area right under the solar plexus, also an aid in protecting that area, along with building a stronger upper abdominal area (rectus abdominis). Do the twist and you will target the side stomach muscles, your oblique's (Note: Fig. #387).

As far as the lower abdominal area, I recommend leg raises on or off the bench (Note: Fig. #388, #389). Not neglecting a good workout with the medicine ball, start with a light ball and slowly increase towards a heavier one. This is a great help in preparing the body for punches (Note: Fig. #390, #391).

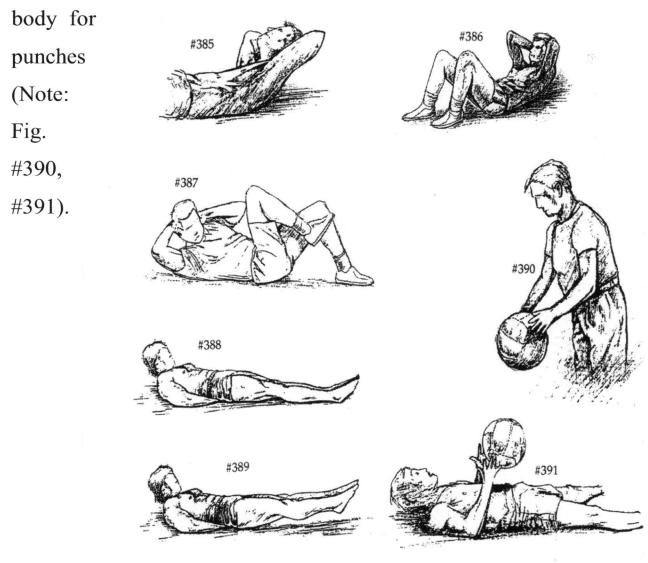

This is a basic workout program, you may have extra needs or if you're lacking in certain areas, for instance, arms, back, chest, stomach, neck, etc., have a professional trainer, physical therapist or a <u>knowledgeable</u> coach assist you in some other exercises for that particular area, and executing <u>proper</u> <u>form</u> while doing them.

While training for a bout that's only 3 weeks away, stop your weight training and switch to calisthenics in place of weight training. Working out with your own body weight (**callisthenic** exercises) <u>this</u> <u>close</u> <u>to</u> <u>a</u> <u>bout</u> will help your coordination, balance speed and punching accuracy. At this time you're <u>not</u> looking to add new muscle to your frame, but we still need to <u>maintain</u> the muscle we already have, calisthenics will do this. Keeping in line with the workout routine in chapter 9, we will work out the same muscle areas <u>without</u> weights. This workout or a similar one could be utilized in place of weight training if you're personally against weight training, or favor calisthenics.

Day 1 -   <u>Triceps</u> and <u>shoulders</u>, do behind the back pushups (Note: Fig. #392 - #393), 2-3 sets. Dips, they could also be done in between two chairs as shown if dipping bars are not available, not leaning forward will target the triceps and shoulders most (Note: Fig. #394, #395), 2-3 sets of as many as you can do, plus 1 more…

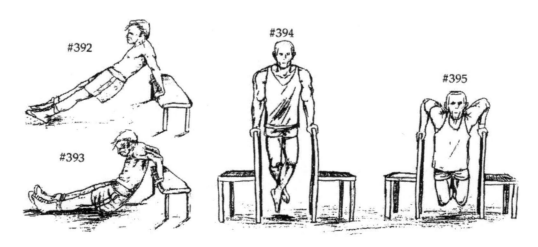

Day 2 -<u>Back</u> and <u>neck</u>, do pull-ups front 2-3 sets as many as you can, and 1 more! **If I don't place a number of reps on the exercise always do as many as you can plus one more.**

(Note: Fig. #396, #397) and pull-ups behind the neck 2-3 sets (Note: Fig. #398, #399). For your neck just do neck movements left and right, front & back to keep the neck loose but ready.

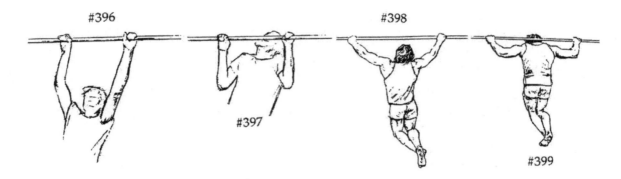

Day 3 -   OFF

Day 4 -   <u>Chest</u> and <u>biceps</u>, chin-ups 2 sets (Note: Fig. #400, #401). Do regular pushups 3 sets, your body should be kept straight throughout this exercise. (Note: Fig. #402, #403).

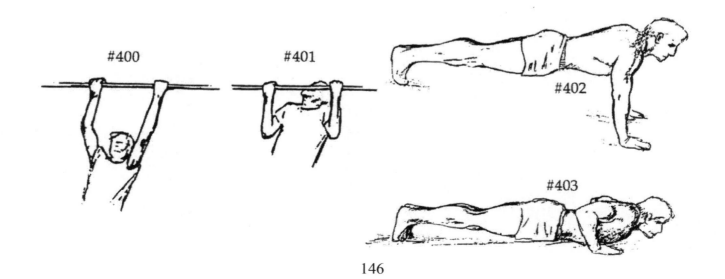

Day 5 - OFF

Day 6 - <u>Legs</u>, free squats, (squats without weight) placing a board under your heels may help you balance. Remember to keep your body upright and your back straight throughout this exercise, 2 sets (Note: Fig. #404, #405).

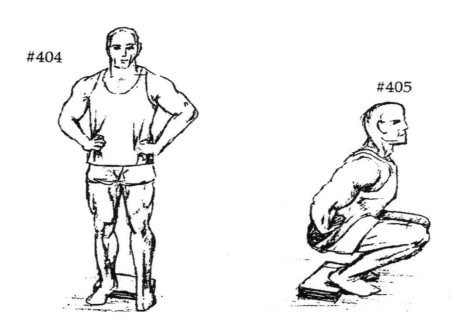

#404

#405

Day 7 – OFF

This is in <u>addition</u> to your regular boxing workout. Remember do all exercises to <u>failure</u> (when you cannot do another rep) and keep your rest in between sets to about 1-3 minutes.

The <u>last</u> <u>3</u> <u>days</u> **before any bout**, limit workouts to <u>only</u> light stretching and stomach exercises, increasing your shadow boxing and resting. <u>Stop</u> all sparring, running, bag hitting, weight lifting, and calisthenics.

Chapter 10

* GENERAL HEALTH *

Running, will work the largest muscles in the body, therefore, burning the most calories than you would working any other muscle group. Running not only will help to rid your body of unwanted fat, it builds endurance and stamina. Run, preferably on an empty stomach, and a soft track. If you have weak knees try running on a treadmill, and always wear a good pair of running shoes. When running on a treadmill use a slight incline, remember "life is an uphill climb" so prepare yourself. Walking briskly at 3.3 – 4.4 m.p.h. on your treadmill and throwing punches simultaneously as a warm-up or cool-down will increase your sense of balance control. Since the ground is moving you will not be able to stop and punch as you might when running on solid ground, try it!

When I was young, I remember reading that boxers ran wearing combat boots, and that this would help to strengthen the legs, well I started doing that and suffered pulled ligaments in both knees! For six months I couldn't run, each boot weighed 5lbs! Learn through my mistake, never run with weights on your feet. To build up your legs work out with weights, but not while you're running!

(Note: Fig. #406).

#406

Running 10-20 miles a day will only help you if you're training to run 10-20 miles. If your training for boxing, concentrate on training for the three minute duration (the round), then rest the one minute (the rest period). Sprint the three minutes or run as fast as possible, then rest one minute and so on. Try to cover more ground each time during your sprint. After your sprinting exercise, run or jog 1-2 miles to cool down. Remember, you don't want to leave yourself tired, spent or used up with your running exercise alone!

If you suffer from back pain before or after running try waiting one hour after you wake up, before the running portion of your workout. While you're asleep, fluids build in the spinal disc causing the lower back to be tense and sensitive to irritation. Remember to always <u>warm up first</u>, then stretch, before doing any running or exercise.

As far as shaping or toning muscles is concerned, muscle tone is a measure of the healthy tension in a conditional muscle while at rest. Practically any type of exercise will do this, but this cannot be done without building muscle. The <u>bigger the muscle</u> and the <u>less body fat</u> you have, determines the bodies firmness, tone, shape or whatever you want to call it, it's really called building muscle!

If you're dieting in an attempt to lose fat, weight training is of great importance, helping to offset the negative loss of muscle that goes along with losing weight! Some fighters I know, I won't mention any names, literally blow up when not in training, then when they sign for a fight, they will try to lose all of their excess fat they accumulated in between fights. In a few short weeks, along with their loss, they most certainly lose muscle tissue (Note: Fig. #407). If you're a fighter, never let your weight go beyond eight pounds of your true fighting weight. This way, if you have to fight within a few weeks or so, you will have time to train properly, honing your skills, timing and reflexes not just running and dieting!

Nutrition is the single most important equation in the life of an athlete or anyone interested in becoming one, "you are what you eat" (Note: Fig. #408). This holds true, the boxers eating pattern should be one that reduces body fat and builds lean muscle. To do this you need to adhere to a diet rich in nutrients and low in calories and fat. Fat when digested, deposits quickly to stored fat in our bodies! In fact, the rewards of an extremely low-fat diet are enormous; not only benefiting your overall appearance but also helping to ward off hypertension, heart attacks, diabetes and cancer!

Protein and carbohydrate intake in your diet should total 1 to 1.25 grams of protein per pound of your body weight daily. Too many calories beyond what your body uses even if they are carbohydrates will lead to body fat. So, avoid high calorie, high carbohydrate and high sugar foods, they will all make you gain fat not muscle!

#407   #408

Read all labels thoroughly before making any food or supplement selections. Many advertised foods that state they're "fat free" are not, "light" meats and cheeses often still get most of their calories from fat. I had the privilege to meet Jack LaLanne and I asked him personally, I asked him, "Jack what advice can you give me as far as eating right?" He replied, "Joseph, if its man-made don't eat it; if you can't pronounce it, don't eat it; read labels on food."

To find approximately how many calories you should be digesting to maintain your current body weight, multiply your weight by 20, example: I weight 170lbs, 20 X 170 = 3400 calories.

If you're not "very active" multiply your weight by only 15, example: 170 X 15=2550 calories. Whichever, or whatever your amount comes to, this should be the amount at which you do not lose or gain fat. This formula is only approximate; you may have to experiment to exactly find your own maintenance caloric intake.

To lose body fat, you might try fluctuating your caloric intake, for instance, you may try consuming your regular amount of calories (this is the amount of calories that will not make you gain or lose weight) 3 days one week, on the other 4 days try consuming anywhere from 750 to 1000 calories <u>less</u>, alternating days, or simply flip a coin at the beginning of each day heads all of your regular calorie intake and if it's tails, your sub maintenance calorie intake, 750-1000 calories less. By doing this you're tricking your body keeping it from lowering its metabolic rate.

Example; if you were to diet or skip a couple of meals, your body thinks you're starving it. Your body in turn will slow down your metabolism to conserve energy. When eating your next meal your body conserves a large number of calories, from that meal as fat and stores them to prepare for the next famine, this is our body's response. So, if you skip meals, or eat one very large meal a day you fit into this category. If you want to eat more food, more often and lose weight, read on!

I don't recommend trying any low calorie diet plans, commercial diet programs, or diet shakes; just vary your daily calorie intake. I recommend chewing most of your meals not drinking them! Once again, because it's worth repeating calorie restricting diets slow down the rate of which you burn fat by having your body's metabolism slow down, many a time you may lose some weight, but the weight you will lose will soon return, once your normal eating habits return!

What's really important is to change your eating habits and increase your metabolism permanently, by exercising and eating small well balanced meals often. Eating meals too late in the day will only turn to fat, try eating the last meal of your day no later than 5 hours before retiring for the night. Remember, you don't need energy to fall asleep, if in need of a snack, make it a cup of organic spinach or a hardboiled egg with some water. Don't eat starches late at night, they're the most complex of carbohydrates, taking the longest to digest and turn to energy, ingesting them early in the day is most favorable. To understand all of what I have written on the subject of nutrition, purchase a calorie counting book, one that also includes the counting of fat, protein and carbohydrate grams. This is a must when you're trying to consume the right foods in the right balance.

I recommend, eating <u>4-6</u> <u>small</u> <u>meals</u> <u>a</u> <u>day</u> <u>spaced</u> <u>every</u> <u>2-3</u> <u>hours</u> apart, having each meal consist of 60% of its calories from carbohydrates like beans, rice, potatoes, pasta, vegetables, fruit and whole grain breads and oatmeal, 30% from proteins like fish, or turkey (without the skin), lean red meat, or grass fed lean ground beef, or substitute lean ground turkey for ground beef, egg whites or protein powder if you have it. Remember, trim all visible fat from meat and turkey before cooking and before eating, also draining any excess fats as your cooking.

With the remaining balance, of only 10% of your meals calories from fat. Which translates to about <u>25</u> <u>grams</u> <u>of</u> <u>fat</u> <u>per</u> <u>day</u>. Ingesting 40-100 grams of carbohydrates within 15-30 minutes after your workout and ingesting 40-60 grams of protein within 90 minutes after your workout. Doing this, will give your muscles the nourishment they need, when they need it most!

Replacing the usual three good sized meals, with these 4-6 smaller ones, you're keeping your body nourished throughout the day. This will aid in the recuperative process, rebuilding the broken down muscles caused by your intense workouts. No, you're not training to become a sumo wrestler! These are <u>small</u> meals like a tuna sandwich (packed in water) on whole wheat bread, some vegetables, a banana or an apple and a tall glass of water would be considered one of these small meals. Don't eat simply because you're hungry; eat because the clock say's it's time to eat! Smaller meals will aid in speeding up your metabolism, along with your weight training and aerobic workouts. This will not only help you gain strength and muscle, but lose excess body fat at the <u>same</u> <u>time</u>! Remember, nutritional meals means plenty of fruits and vegetables, (not canned but frozen is alright) fresh is best. The vegetables can be eaten raw, lightly steamed, cooked in the oven or toaster oven. Eat at least 5 servings of fruits and vegetables every day. A serving consist of ½ cup of fruit, and ½ cup cut vegetables, 1 cup of leafy vegetables, ¼ cup dried fruit or ½ cup nuts/beans. Note: Please be aware and limit your sugar intake re: all foods that you consume. Keep sugar and sodium intake as low as possible, stay away from processed foods, artificial colors, artificial flavorings, artificial sweeteners, high-fructose corn syrup, preservatives, trans fats, GMO's, sodium nitrites/nitrates, growth hormones, MSG, BHA, BHT, antibiotics, pesticides and herbicides.

Making small changes in your eating habits <u>can</u> <u>and</u> <u>will</u> make a positive difference in your health. <u>Don't</u> eat cakes, candy, candy bars, sodas or greasy foods and stay away from fast food restaurants and drive-thru. Eating smarter doesn't always require that you spend more money, just that you plan better and become more <u>informed</u>!

For starters, roast, bake, broil, and boil in place of frying. If frying use an air fryer, it fry's your food without oil. Use coconut oil over all other oils. Make large portions of food and place them in small convenient plastic (BPA/Phthalate free) or glass containers to bring to work, or the gym, or where ever you go. This will assure you of quality food throughout the day and keep you on your eating schedule. You can even freeze them and consume them throughout the week!

<u>Aerobics</u> stimulate the production of fat burning enzymes and the utilization of fat for fuel. There is no better aerobic workout than a good <u>boxing</u> <u>workout</u>! At the end of your boxing workout if you're NOT sweating profusely, short of breath or at least fatigued you need to workout more intensely or go a few more rounds.

To stay in shape or to get in shape, but not as a "real boxer" per se, in essence you can use boxing, as a pure aerobic exercise! Here is a program I put together, with much success! What's needed first is some good fast music, something with an upbeat, music that will continue at least 20-30 minutes, that's a good aerobic start, working up to 40 minutes in about 3-4 weeks.

Start with a 5 minute warm -up and stretch (Note: Fig. #409, #410), then with no resting go right to work on the striking bag for 5 minutes (Note: Fig. #411), then right to the heavy bag pounding away another 5 minutes (Note: Fig. #412), from there to the speed

156

bag, 5 minutes (Note: Fig. #413), and 7 minutes of rope jumping (Note: Fig. #414), and cool down with 3 minutes of shadow boxing (Note: Fig. #415).There are <u>no</u> bells, <u>no</u> rounds, this is done continuously!

You will of course have to pace yourself it's <u>not</u> like working out for boxing, where there are three minute rounds of all out intense work, and one minute rest in between each round. This is an excellent aerobic workout and you don't have to be a boxer to do it, "just do it!" In a few short weeks, you'll see great results in your endurance, waist line and in your all-around well-being, provided of course your fat consumption is at a minimum and your nutritional intake is adequate, give it a try!

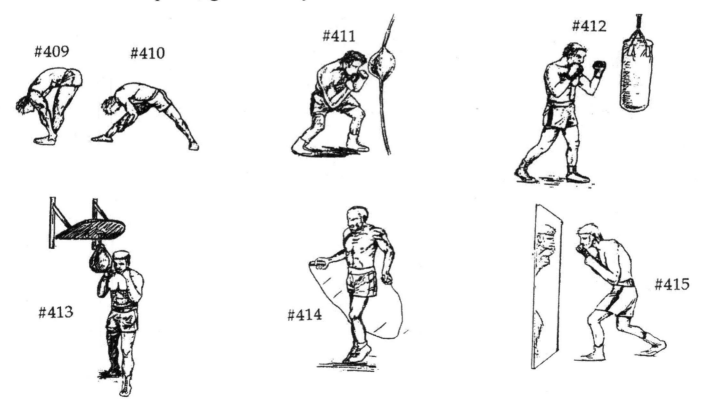

#409 #410 #411 #412 #413 #414 #415

When doing aerobic exercise, especially in the beginning it's important to know your heart rate. To get in shape, your heart must keep beating at 75% to 90% of its capacity during your workout. This is called your (target heart rate) or training zone. To figure out your training zone, subtract your age from 220, multiply that number by the desired rate. For instance, to start, multiply that number by 75% or 0.75, example: if you are "21" years old, 220 – "21" = 199. This 199 would be considered your maximum heart rate; working at this rate would be your 100% capacity.

What we want to do is workout between 75% to 90% of that, this is considered your training zone. The 199 is this person's maximum heart rate. Starting at 75% of this "21" year olds maximum heart rate would be about 149 beats per minute; this would be <u>his</u> training zone. Keeping his heart beating at the 149 beats per minute throughout his entire workout, lasting no <u>less</u> than 22 minutes and no <u>more</u> than 50 minutes he or she will achieve a true aerobic workout, and receive it's full benefit. Raise your target percentage from your starting percentage of 75% towards 90% gradually. Moving your target rate to 90% would of course be more difficult, but will lead to greater fitness gains. Take your time and don't push too hard too soon, remember how to eat that elephant!

To take your pulse during exercise, count the beats on your neck or wrist for 6 seconds, then multiply that number by 10. Having a heart monitor will be an excellent aid in doing this.

The benefits of high repetition exercise are best obtained from aerobic exercises, for example: rope jumping, bag punching, sparring, running, jogging, bicycling, stair climbing, etc. etc. and <u>not</u> weight lifting, save that for muscle growth.

<u>Water</u> is the most important nutrient needed to enhance athletic performance. Water helps regulate your body's temperature through perspiration. Water lubricates all the joints in our body. The more you workout, the more water your body needs to maintain proper fluid balance. Drink water <u>before</u>, <u>during</u> and <u>after</u> all workouts. A loss of only one percent body weight 1% in water will cause a measurable decline in your exercising ability and performance. In fact, sweating off 2% of your weight in water decreases athletic ability 20%! Thirst is a very bad indicator of our bodies need for water; in fact athletes have been known to lose up to five percent of their body weight in water, before they felt thirsty enough to drink. Drink ½ your body weight in ounces of water each day. For instance, my current body weight is 170lbs., this would mean I should be drinking 85 ounces of water daily. Some days I do, some days I don't; when I do my day seems to flow along better and I feel great!

In our busy day to day life style, it sometimes seems difficult or expensive to simply relax and rejuvenate. Furthermore, pollutions of the air, some water supplies and food sources along with a seemingly worsening social environment, drag us all down faster than we can build back up. This makes a strong case for large amounts of natural, raw fruits and vegetables, organically grown if possible, always thoroughly cleaning them first before eating them. Juicing them is also an excellent way to get fruits and vegetables in your diet and in a complete compact format, this is one way I get my greens especially the ones I don't like, and just by adding a few apples and carrots in the juicer. The drink will taste great and it's naturally sweetened! This could be one of your 4-6 meals. Bring it with you to work in a thermos.

Add antioxidants such as Vitamin E, beta carotene and selenium to help combat todays environmental hazards. Some natural antioxidants are fruits, vegetables, whole grains, legumes, olive oil and nuts. Along with a daily vitamin and mineral tablet, one giving you all your daily requirements (I recommend natural over synthetic). Amino acids are the building blocks of protein, make sure you ingest all 21 Amino acids.

Not neglecting herbs, herbs were once a "cure all" centuries ago, are just as real now, and are rapidly replacing drugs, because of their many natural healing abilities. They can give one an ability to bring on and maintain vibrant health, without any bad side effects. This is a strong come back to society as a whole to what is natural and good for us. Remember herbs are <u>foods</u>, not drugs!

Saturated fat and meat consumption should be reduced in our diet, and we should shift toward more foods from plant sources. Vitamins, minerals and herbs <u>all</u> play a big part in our daily life and are vitally important to us, by using them to supplement our daily nutritional intake. Because it's difficult for most of us to simply consume our daily minimum requirements, taking supplements can assure us that we are. Remember supplements are just that, they're not substitutions. Always avoid fat and eat nutritiously!

In short, treat your body like a high performance racing car, it's always properly tuned, well fed and lubricated. So train intensely, eat nutritiously, rest adequately so you won't "break down" and drink plenty of water!

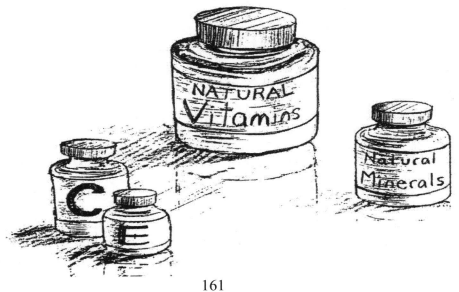

Chapter 11

* WHY THIS BOOK *

With my more than three decades of boxing experience and nine years in the making of this book, this was not going to be a book at all. I originally wrote and had it copy written as a script to be the first boxing video ever, back in 1985. (REFER TO INTRO)

I firmly believe in this book; it has my heart, soul, and knowledge on every page, and it could very well mean the difference between being good or becoming great, but that's all up to you. I didn't write this book to make a large sum of money, although that would be nice. Boxing is what I know, and what I would like to share to those who don't…

When I was younger and studied martial arts, my first teacher was a Kung-Fu master, his name was Tito. Tito taught me the art of Kung-Fu along with the philosophy behind it. There was a time during our training that I could no longer financially afford to continue with our lessons. When I made mention of this to Tito, his response in one I will never forget, and up till this day, is still ringing in my ears. He said, "If you're willing to learn, I'm willing to teach." Well I'm willing to teach boxing, here's the book! "Are you willing to learn?"

Revisit this book and refer to this book regularly, because it's impossible to grasp it all in any one reading. Use it as a guide or a workbook, and highlight areas with a yellow highlighter, areas pertaining to you or that are particularly important to you; things you never want to forget!

This book was written for the "Mr. Average," to help protect himself. It's for the youngster interested in amateur bouts, and then it's also for the professional, who quite honestly wants to become champion of the world!! Use whatever can help you in this book in good health…

Never use your boxing skills to harm anyone outside the ring, this means don't become a bully or a punk. This book was written with self-defense in mind, along with good sportsmanship. Do not abuse your skills or anything learned in this book. Respect all people and learn to understand your ability, and bring an attitude of letting things go. If you have the skill to do damage, this does not mean you should use it anywhere else but in the ring. Try hard to walk away from trouble if you can. Knowing yourself and your capabilities and the knowledge to give a hurting to someone, don't, unless it's used for self-defense. I cannot stress this more. Try to be slow to anger and quick to laugh no matter what the circumstances. It's Proverbs 15:1 (NKJV) "A soft answer turns away wrath but a harsh word stirs up anger." Keep in mind, boxing has been labeled.

"The Noble Art of Self-Defense."

When participating in or practicing martial arts and boxing at the same time both become confusing. Boxing commits the shoulders in its punches, martial arts does not. If you're boxing amateur or professional, martial arts practice will throw you off. You might just kick your opponent, or hit him with a back fist, therefore losing points or being disqualified. Remember, there are only eight punches in boxing, but they could be thrown from <u>infinite</u> <u>angles</u>, with slight <u>variations</u>. Skillfully mastering these boxing punches, combined with the proper footwork turns Clark Kent into "<u>Superman!</u>"

When I was younger my family and I lived in the Manhattanville projects in Harlem, New York City. Remembering back when I was only 7 or 8 years old my dad brought the first pair of boxing gloves home, primarily for my older brothers Bobby and Tony because they wrestled and fought often, like most teenage brothers do. From that day on I was fascinated with the gloves and with boxing. My Dad having boxed in his younger days showed us some of the basics and fundamentals. My older brother Ron used to spar with me on <u>his</u> <u>knees</u> using only <u>one</u> <u>hand</u>, while <u>I</u> <u>was</u> <u>standing</u> <u>using</u> <u>both</u> <u>hands</u>; from then on I was <u>hooked</u>.

Boxing has kept me out of trouble, off the streets, off drugs, off smoking and away from alcohol and in the gym, or training on my own! I also credit boxing for bestowing upon me the confidence, discipline and drive needed on becoming self-employed and self-supporting since I was 19 years old, Thank God for Boxing!

Being an avid student of boxing, and having a great interest in boxing's old fight films, helped me to comprehend and analyze the many fighting styles and each ones strengths and weaknesses.

As an aid to understanding and mastering the many boxing moves and techniques in this book, consider having someone videotape <u>your</u> workout, shadow boxing and later sparring. This is a remarkably helpful tool for learning and practicing proper technique. Make sure you have someone view the video, who knows what to look for, and how to correct your faults. It will also be useful to have your entire workout videotaped. The weight training segment as well as all bag punching and rope jumping, do this every three months.

Be aware of your form when lifting the weights, correcting any faults. While punching the bags look for the dropping of your guard, throwing all punches correctly, returning your punches correctly, proper foot placement, the turning of your hips into all power punches, omitting all slow and lazy punches etc. etc... Work towards improving further and perfecting your skills, dropping any bad habits you may have picked up along the way (Note: Fig. #416).

#416

You should work out every day for boxing; if boxing is what you want to improve upon. This means shadow boxing and learning and practicing all the boxing moves, towards an all-out attempt to master them. Remember, train for your sport, it's good to play other sports as an aid to yours to break the monotony. For instance, handball is a great game for boxing, it uses both hands in a way that duplicates punching movements, improves eye-hand coordination, reflexes and body placement. Paddleball and racquetball are also an aid to boxing movements.

The great basketball player plays basketball to become great. The great golfer plays golf to become great. Get the picture! Break the monotony from time to time, but if your goal is to become "great" in boxing you have to train for boxing, eat for boxing, run for boxing, and sleep for boxing.

Adequate sleep is very important; this is when your body recuperates from your day. Some people need more sleep than others, if you find yourself falling asleep at traffic lights, while you're driving, you need more! You might say "I don't have enough time to workout!" Add a month or more to each of your years, by simply waking up one hour or so earlier each day! Accomplish this by going to sleep earlier; this will give you the extra productive time you may need to achieve whatever you "can't get done." Don't try staying up later at night; it's easier to be more productive in the morning than late at night! Get your needed rest but don't be ridiculous, especially on days off or weekends, wake up early! Don't be a bed bum! Get up! Do something more with your life; <u>whatever</u> that may be.

Don't waste the precious time you have! Be productive at all times and <u>always</u> <u>make</u> time for your workouts! Sleeping past what your body actually needs to recuperate will be counterproductive, meaning the more sleep you may get, the worse you will feel! There is no such thing as catching up on sleep! Get your 7-8 hours if needed and get back to living! If your training is intense and often you may need an afternoon nap of an hour or so, some fighters do and some don't. Sleeping is for dreaming, life is reality, wake up and get real! No drugs! No drinking alcohol! No smoking of any kind!

I can relate a boxing match, or boxing training to riding a motorcycle in N.Y.C. traffic! This is not the time or place to be lackadaisical or sluggish, you must be consistently alert! At your best, and wide awake! Use this analogy in <u>your</u> training and fighting.

Remember, what may work for an unmarried, unemployed well rested man in his twenties who is properly nourished and stress free, will fail to work for a man in his thirties or forties that's married with children, works 6 days a week, cuts corners in his diet and is highly stressed from all directions. You must <u>listen</u> to <u>your</u> body and <u>tailor</u> <u>your</u> training accordingly. A major part in muscle growth, increased energy and progress with your workouts, is to <u>know</u> when to <u>cut</u> <u>back</u> on your training and to constantly supply your body with the steady <u>nutritional</u> meals it needs. Not forgetting to drink half of your body weight in ounces of <u>water</u> each day, combined with adequate <u>rest</u> so your body <u>will</u> repair itself and grow, and your workouts <u>will</u> advance.

If you're a full time boxer without other work, working out 3 times daily is best. Workouts must not exceed the 50 minute limit! <u>First</u>, workout in the A.M. running and stomach exercises, do this on an empty stomach. <u>Second</u>, if it's a weight training day your weight training workout will be about 3-5 hours after your running & stomach exercises. <u>Third</u> and last; your boxing workout, about 3-5 hours after your weight training workout.

If it's an <u>off</u> day for weight training or you prefer not to work out with weights, do your <u>boxing</u> <u>work</u> <u>out</u> <u>earlier</u>. Rest and recuperate and eat properly. <u>Always warm up first</u>! Work outs could go like this...

Monday – A.M. running & stomach exercises
Afternoon, weight training
Early P.M. boxing work out.

Tuesday – A.M. running & stomach exercises
Afternoon, weight training
Early P.M. boxing work out.

Wednesday – A.M. running & stomach exercises
Afternoon or early P.M. boxing work out.

Thursday – A.M. running & stomach exercises
Afternoon, weight training
Early P.M. boxing work out.

Friday – A.M. running & stomach exercises
Afternoon or early P.M. boxing work out.

Saturday – A.M. running & stomach exercises
Afternoon, weight training
Early P.M. boxing work out.

Sunday – OFF (Frequent a Church that teaches the Bible)

If you work full time, try to get up early enough to do your running and stomach exercises, then shower, go to work and remember your <u>meals</u> and <u>water</u> consumption during the day. After work you can work out at the gym or at home. Try alternating days, one day your boxing work out the next day your weight training or callisthenic work out, or try doing your boxing work out, then a light calisthenics work out combined daily. The <u>choice</u> is <u>all</u> yours, after your work out eat and relax.

Boxing is the ability to outsmart an opponent and out maneuver him. I don't recommend exchanging punch for punch with any fighter, "Boxing is a skill to hit and <u>not</u> get hit." You punch where he is and he punches where you were! Boxing uses mind over matter, using <u>learned</u> refined boxing skills and that's the science of the sport of boxing. To obtain this ability and move beyond the simplistic to more serious levels of mastery, you must understand the fundamentals, the basics, the different types of punches, the moves, the <u>when</u>, <u>where</u> and the <u>how</u> each move is best put into use. Practice to develop combinations of punches that will work on various opponents; all this is up to you and is obtainable so go for it!

Chapter 12

* MOTIVATION *

Here is a little poem I wrote, entitled, "If you were Clever"

Don't waste energy, but be prepared too

Don't throw more punches than are needed, but be able to

Don't run farther than you have to, but know you can if you need to

Don't take punishment, not ever

Don't trade punches if you're clever, if you're clever.

Stay clear of all negative people and negative situations. Your mind should be filled with thoughts of progress and success! Seek your dream! If you want to be part of the precious few who become great champions, here are the ingredients. First, I would place God, The God of The Bible, Jesus is God; then there's motivation, this is the single most vital ingredients that no one can give you, but you! Find what motivates you and use it. Second, there's confidence, confidence in you.

This comes by doing your homework and being in top condition! Third, there's knowledge, knowledge is power! Use whatever you can learn from **this book** and any other source to bring you closer to your dream. Forth, there's the will to win, yes you have to want it very bad! Bad enough to hold out past the pain of training, the agony of sacrifice, through the relentless pursuit of fighting perfection and the seclusion this may bring, mix it all up with the problems and commitments of your personal and everyday life. Throw in the stress that all this puts your mind and body through; this is the road to take in becoming a champion.

Yes, you must be hungry for victory to claim it! But, you <u>can</u> still do it! Put yourself in charge of yourself! Be all you can be! If you love boxing, you should give yourself a chance to see how far you can really go with it! You might ask yourself "Am I too old for professional boxing?" The answer is, "How old do you feel?" Mark Twain may have said it best when he said, "Age is a matter of mind, if you don't mind, it doesn't matter." It's how good you feel and how well you perform in the boxing ring that counts, not the year you were born. I know of many past great fighters that fought well into their forties, many not admitting their real age, some possibly in their early fifties. In the past there were world class fighters that were past their "prime boxing years" but still going strong. To name just a few; Larry Holmes, George Foreman, Evander Holyfield, Thomas Hearns, Alexis Arguello, Roberto Duran, Bernard Hopkins, Archie Moore, and Antonio Tarver.

Let's say you're thirty years old, but you're not sure if you have reached <u>your</u> prime yet, ten years passed and your now forty years old. You feel you have just reached <u>your</u> prime, you can do things you couldn't do at twenty you feel faster, stronger and have more endurance, or maybe just more experience and skill. Either way, believing it may very well make it so. Not believing it, makes it not probable at all. Believe in your hard-earned abilities, if their real; if not you will find out soon enough.

Here's one more example: Let's say your 40 years old, but you have never trained hard enough, or long enough or knew enough to reach your personal best condition. The time comes when you devote all your efforts to training with new knowledge and greater motivation and you reach a peak in your condition and abilities, one that you have never dreamed of, but yet it happens! Who could possibly argue with you on such a matter, it may or may not be true. Some men peak at twenty some thirty some forty. Let your performance or lack of it, personally inform you, when you should "hang them up." So, to answer the question; I would say if you're fifty years old, don't start a professional boxing career as a fighter, but you can always learn to be a boxing trainer or manager and definitely keep working out, don't give up on YOU!

You may not want to box in the ring on any level, but the workouts can't be beat! You may ask yourself "Am I too young to start training for boxing?" The answer is "How young do you feel?" I started training when I was 7 or 8 years old, thanks to my brother Robert's influence and example. Working out and training can start whenever and should continue throughout your entire life! It will keep you young, energetic, along with physically and mentally alert!

I remember this bout I had many years ago. It was in the New York City Golden Gloves. In amateur boxing early on, you never know who you're going to have to fight. Well this day started out with my trainer not showing up, but I ran into a friend I knew and trained with in the gym. He was the best light weight in The Police Athletes League (PAL) and the New York City amateur champion and was also undefeated. We had worked out together many times, but never sparred each other.

On this day he forgot his mouthpiece and asked if he could borrow mine, I replied, "Ok, no problem" I then added "If our trainer doesn't arrive can you assist in my corner" he replied "Definitely, if you would do the same for me" I said "I would be honored to." Then he asked me if I was feeling alright, well he noticed I looked kind of run down. I was, I told him it was because I must have caught a cold or the flu, I had a fever also. I remember I had worked delivering milk the night before and couldn't get any sleep. I also was overweight by 3 or 4 pounds for the weight class that I had signed up for (light weight) and it was too late to change it. Also there were only 6 weight classes back then, today there are 17, Seventeen!

So all during that day I wore a plastic sweat suit and I stayed in the bathroom with the shower water running as hot as possible. I was trying to lose some weight, an hour and a half of throwing punches with the suit on and hot water steaming up all around me, I had lost 1 pound. It seemed that I just couldn't lose any more weight. I also didn't have anything to drink all day until after the weigh-in, about 10 minutes before seeing my friend.

At the event the boxing delegate said it was alright to fight, but to try to lose more weight. It was a good thing they didn't take my temperature! They posted the fighters names on a billboard, hanging on a wall in a large hallway, my name appeared alongside my friend's name. We both couldn't believe it, neither one of us wanted to fight the other. We both went back to the boxing delegate at the event and told him we trained together, we were friends, we're from the same gym and we're not fighting each other. And I asked for him to please change it, so we may fight some other fighters. He said he would not and if we didn't want to fight each other we would both be disqualified! We were both in shock; we realized that we really had to fight one another. We couldn't talk to each other after that; we were both in a daze. We just wished each other good luck and walked in different directions until the fight began.

I felt I was about 50% of myself; I definitely was not at my best to say the least. Because of my fever and weakness, the work the night before, the not sleeping and trying to lose weight as I did, along with the fact I was fighting the best fighter in New York, in my weight class and my trainer was not there, but I still wanted to fight anyway. I wasn't looking for any excuses but these were the facts. I didn't want to let myself, my friends or family down. They were out there in the crowd waiting for <u>my</u> fight. My friend definitely was going to fight, he didn't come to the event to go home without fighting or be disqualified because of me.

When our fight time came, we got into the ring and because our trainer wasn't there that day, remember we had the same trainer. So, in my friends corner, was the assistant trainer from our gym and there was only one assistant and he was a closer friend to my opponent, so in my corner I had no one! So I asked my brother-in-law, from the audience to assist me in the corner and he reluctantly did. He said he knew nothing, and I knew that. I said just put the stool in the ring when the bell rings, and don't worry, it will be okay. There I was, the cards stacked against me. Physically I was 50% or less than my true self, I was seconds away from fighting a great fighter with an inexperienced man in my corner. The bell rang, Round 1: We both danced in the middle of the ring, we showboated, we feinted, we moved swiftly and elusively, but we did not punch each other once, we were friends. We also respected each other too much and knew each other's true abilities.

My friend was 100% and I wasn't, I knew this and because he was my friend he also knew it. I also knew deep within myself I have this will to win, my psychological side takes over and tells me not to let go! This <u>inner</u> <u>determination</u> or mental power that drives me to overcome my poor physical condition, and use my knowledge, my skill, my confidence, my heart and relentless determination to overcome that 50% loss of energy and strength. Well, Round 2: came quickly, and we both realized that we had to give it our all and try to win! So we both did, it was for real! Neither one of us were going to lay down for the other! Then came Round 3: the final round and we both fought our hearts out and I was awarded the decision on the scorecards cards; as I out punched my opponent and landed more punches to gain that victory.

After the fight, in the same hallway where the names were posted, we came together once again. I said to my friend "I had just beaten the best there is, I cannot lose this Golden Glove title," he thanked me and said, "It was a good fight and the best man won." Yes we were still friends, but we lost touch with each other after that night and I never saw him again. I won the next bout at Sunny Side Gardens in Queens N.Y. easily but that year I was disqualified right before the semi-final bout, because of 2 extra pounds I couldn't remove from my body. I definitely was in the wrong weight class, but back then there were only 6 weight classes to choose from.

The point here is <u>boxing</u> is <u>50%</u> (<u>psychological</u> <u>or</u> <u>mental</u>) and <u>50%</u> (<u>physical</u>). Yes, you need to be in the best physical condition possible, but you also have to want it badly! Believing deep in your heart you can't be beat, really believing you are the best, in spite of the odds, knowing yourself and your abilities and having the confidence to <u>not</u> <u>ever</u> give up. With this knowledge and drive to succeed you will!

Before big championship fights, both fighters are always interviewed. The fighter who's always saying "I will give him a good fight" or "I will try my best" or "I have a good chance" this fighter is already the loser! Have confidence and believe deep within your heart that you will win! If you believe otherwise you're not ready for that fight!

On that night in N.Y. inside that boxing ring, I simply wanted to win more than my friend did, you see, he had the tools to beat me, but I didn't want him too! I wouldn't give into my poor condition. I told myself I am the best, and I <u>will</u> win! Losing should <u>never</u> enter your mind! I used my mental mindset to overcome my physical condition. This I what makes champions, champions. Hone up on your drive and commitment. How bad do you want it? That's how hard you will try; don't give up on yourself <u>ever</u>!

Sometimes your true innate abilities are hidden deep within you. When on the outside most things <u>may</u> seem impossible, deep within you, there's an "Inner Determination" once exposed and <u>tapped</u> into, can perform miracles! I never believed I would ever finish this book. I started writing the first page almost a decade ago, I worked on it 16 hours a day for weeks and weeks and weeks to the books end, and to me it's a miracle just to <u>finish</u> it! I tapped into this hidden ability that we all have; if you want something bad enough, tap into it, by not letting go! Don't give up your dreams! Whatever they may be, Big or Small!!

If you tried hard, read and practiced everything in this book thoroughly highlighting areas important to you, tried <u>different</u> trainers and you're still disappointed in your lack of boxing ability. Then it might not be in the cards for you to become a boxing professional, or even compete in boxing on any level. Learn what you can from boxing and move on. Use boxing and it's training to help you go through your everyday life. It builds confidence, enhances perseverance, increases strength, reduces stress, gives you more vitality, helps to combat depression, improves your appearance, enhances your sex life, besides the endless hidden health benefits this training provides and could very well help you to succeed in any walk of life.

If nothing else use my book to help motivate you. This motivation could lead you into working out; this training will become a <u>GOOD</u> <u>HABIT</u> that will keep you young and strong always! You could be a "white collar boxer" doing all the training for boxing, maybe even some light sparring or maybe not, with no actual bouts, give it a try!

Most times the people closest to you will give you the least encouragement, they'll never tell you that you're doing well and to keep it up! You look stronger and faster than before or that you're in good shape or even ask if they could help in your endeavors, encouraging you in your dreams, being in your corner of hope. They may be, relatives or friends of yours that think you're working out could wait or it should be put off for other things they think are more important, more important to them! They'll say make an exception. A few times you should, but if you stack too many of these *few times* or exceptions together, working out will become the exception!

Make working out and eating properly the rule and not the exception! Yes, the same thing applies to your eating schedule. Be kind with friends and relatives but at the same time be firm, explain the seriousness of your regular workout and nutritional program. Learn to say <u>NO</u> to requests that are inconsistent with <u>your</u> goals! Seek out a <u>supportive</u> environment of friends and relatives. Steer clear of those who cast a negative light on you and your goals, "Don't give them the time of day."

At first, be complete only with yourself to be the best <u>you</u> can be! Set reasonable and attainable goals that will motivate you to work hard. When you achieve these goals, reward yourself somehow. Go out to dinner, buy yourself something or simply go to a movie and don't ever forget to have some honest wholesome fun!

Sometimes the pressure at home may be causing you to train at much less than your full capacity. You may have to move away to a boxing camp or somewhere else to train properly or make a firm commitment with your spouse and/or family members to allow you your much needed time to train with their full cooperation aiding you in your endeavors. Many boxers go away to boxing camps to train because the seclusion and the focus towards the task at hand bring out the best in their abilities. If you can train uninterrupted, while honing your skills and efforts, getting into a "zone" an area where you're totally focused and in harmony with your mind, spirit and body all acting one. Then your training is on the mark and you're in the right environment.

If it appears you're not getting any outside encouragement then look within yourself to find peace with your improvements and keep working out! I cannot stress this more – "Keep on Keeping on!" "Don't Quit!" Practice! Practice! Practice! Don't Quit!

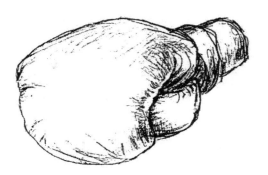

This reminds me of an old poem I didn't write, but I referred to often, entitled **"Don't Quit"**

When things go wrong, as they sometimes will,
When the road you're trudging seems all up hill,
When the funds are low and the debts are high,
And you want to smile, but you have to sigh,
When care is pressing you down a bit,
Rest, if you must – But don't you quit!
Life is peculiar with its twists and turns,
As every one of us sometimes learns,
And many a failure turns about
When he might have won had he stuck it out;
Don't give up, though the pace seems slow
You might succeed with another blow.
Often the goal is nearer than
It seems to a faint and faltering man,
Often the struggler has given up
When he might have captured the victor's cup
And he learned too late, when the night slipped down,
How close he was to the golden crown!
Success is failure turned inside out
The silver tint of the clouds of doubt
And you never can tell how close you are,
It may be so near when it seems so far;
So stick to the fight when you're hardest hit.
It's when things seem worse that you mustn't quit…

CLOSING

I want to thank you for reading through the entire book from the introduction to this closing page. I have poured my heart, sweat and blood at times into writing this book. It has taken considerable time, study, and hands on experience to complete it. I know it will help you greatly if you heed its advice. Read and **study** it, don't just read it. It is best to read it at least 2-3 times and use a highlighter as well. Practice past when it hurts and drive yourself towards excellence as one who learns and perfects the "Sweet Science of Boxing". When I first wrote this book, I was not a Christian, I didn't know God. Yet I told others I did; I was a "Make Believer" I deceived many unknowingly in my profession of faith. I beseech you the reader to cry out to the One who matters the most, Jesus. The first book to read in the Bible should be The Gospel of John. Life is short, and full of troubles; you will seem invincible when in shape, but without Jesus, life is hollow and void. I found this out the hard way. But I also found out, God is Good. I will enclose a poem that I wrote; it's in the book "God's Clarity Through Poetry 2" which explains and displays my conversion, in Christ. It's a true story of how I was Saved from myself, my sins and God's Wrath. I have also written "Digging Deeper into God's Truth Defines a Christian" these books are also available on-line. Happy reading and may God Bless you in countless ways.

Poem Summary

The Poem you are about to read, is the true account of my Christian conversion. I was alone in pain crying out to a "God I thought I knew." When you read this Poem you will be reading how God opened my eyes, softened my heart, converted my mind and soul, awakening me from being Spiritually dead to being Spiritually alive in Him; it happened in a blink of an eye. He has given me a thirst for His Word and His Truths. The morning after that life changing night, went like this…

The next morning I reached out to a Christian friend by phone, the very moment I awoke; while still sitting at my bedside; the first question I asked him was how do you study the Bible? He asked me if I had a Bible Concordance; my reply to him was, whatever that is, I will meet you in 45 minutes at the book store to get one…the rest is History…

God I thought I Knew *(My Testimony)*

On my knees desperately broken, crying out loud, out loud to a God I thought I knew, but didn't…

I cried hard "take my life I have done nothing good with it"…nothing seemed to fit…

I cried and cried endless tears falling down my face, for my family gone, my shame, my guilt, my sin, knowing nothing would be the same, my life totally misplaced, but unbeknownst to me, there was much more I could not see…that would soon, take place…

I cried out "take my life I have done nothing good with it," as my tears fell like heavy rain, I moaned and suffered with each grieving tear drop, greater and greater pain…

Alone in my anguish, sobbing uncontrollably, crying out loud to a God I thought I knew, but didn't…Unbeknownst to me…

I thought I was reaching out for God to hear me…but He was reaching down to me to be heard…

He said, "Read The Bible…Read My Word."

I clearly unmistakably heard…with my ears, my heart or a spiritual part? In the body or out…only God knows…

As chills rolled up and down my spine…was this all in my mind? No…I was in deep awe, and today I am still in it…a total surprise…as my tears immediately stopped flowing from my eyes…my heart skipped a beat, my eyes widened…Who, did I just meet?

I became quiet and still, it was clear to see…His Peace overcame me…

I was spiritually dead, until He said, what He said…

That night I went to sleep with calm I never ever knew…woke with a Biblical thirst, so miraculously anew…

He Called me…now I do clearly perceive what I could never ever on my own…know, desire, or hunger to believe …

His plan for me that night, to un-blind me and give me His clear sight…up to then, I lived recklessly through my foolish self-induced misery…crying out to a God I thought I knew…but didn't…Pretending to be a true believer but all the while, a self-deceiver…a make believer…

I am now all His, and His Good News I do tell…His Mercy Saved me from myself…and from an eternal Hell…

Although that night, I begged Him to take, take my life…and, He did…

He took my old life and gave me New Life in Him…and took away my sin…I am now Born Again…through Grace by Him.

This is my testimony so true…the night I cried out…cried out to a God, I thought I knew…

Ephesians 2:8-9 NKJV

For by grace you have been saved through faith, and that not of yourselves; it is the gift of God, not of works, lest anyone should boast.

Chapter 13

* THE ORIGINAL MARQUESS OF QUEENSBERRY RULES *

From 1866, with some slight variations are still in effect today.

Rule 1. To be fair stand-up boxing match in a twenty four foot ring or as near that size as practicable.

Rule 2. No wrestling or hugging allowed.

Rule 3. The rounds to be of three minute durations and one minute time between rounds.

Rule 4. If either man fall through weakness or otherwise, he must get up unassisted, ten seconds to be allowed him to do so, the other man meanwhile to return to his corner and when the fallen man is on his legs the round to be resumed and continued till the three minutes have expired. If one fails to come to the scratch in the ten seconds allowed, it shall be the referee to give his award in favor of the other man.

Rule 5. A man hanging on the ropes in a helpless state, with his toes off the ground, shall be considered down.

Rule 6. No seconds or any other person to be allowed in the ring during the rounds.

Rule 7.   Should the contest be stopped by an unavoidable interference, the referee to name the time and place as soon as possible for finishing the contest, so that the match must be won and lost, unless the backers of the man agree to draw the stakes.

Rule 8.   The gloves to be fair sized boxing gloves of the best quality and new.

Rule 9.   Should a glove burst, or come off, it must be replaced to the referee's satisfaction

Rule 10.   A man on one knee is considered down and if struck is entitled to the stakes.

Rule 11.   No shoes or boots with springs allowed.

Rule 12.   The contest in all other respects to be governed by the revised rules of the London prize ring.

NOTES

Printed in Great Britain
by Amazon